Politico's Guide to Local Government

To Rafael

Politico's Guide to

Local
Government

Second edition

Andrew Stevens

POLITICO'S

First published in Great Britain 2003 by Politico's Publishing

Second edition published 2006 by
Politico's Publishing, an imprint of
Methuen Publishing Ltd
11–12 Buckingham Gate
London
SW1E 6LB

10 9 8 7 6 5 4 3 2 1

Copyright © Andrew Stevens 2006

A CIP catalogue record for this book is available from the British Library.

ISBN-10: 1-84275-164-6
ISBN-13: 978-1-84275-164-0

Typeset by SX Composing DTP, Rayleigh, Essex
Printed and bound in Great Britain by Cromwell Press, Trowbridge, Wiltshire

Contents

Preface

Since the first edition of the *Politico's Guide to Local Government* was published in 2003, inevitably much has changed on the local government landscape, both in terms of central government policy and actual delivered change. These three years have also given me an opportunity to reflect on the approach of the first edition and how this has been received by the intended audience. Since some of the text in the first edition was a personal rumination on the state of local government at that moment in time, for the second edition I have concentrated on information and topic areas most of use to those in the professions or those studying local government (for instance, those taking NCTJ courses). A more apt title for it might be a 'Guide to Local Governance' or a 'Guide to Local Public Services', as local government is fast becoming a historical footnote in British politics.

In terms of texts sourced in the writing of this edition, where possible I have used the most recent and only referred to older works for historical context (as listed in the Bibliography). The local government publishing field is not what it used to be, though a dwindling yet sufficient range of texts are still produced each year to cater for the market.

With regard to the content, the book primarily covers councils in England and Wales, though there are notes on Scottish, Welsh and

Northern Irish local government in the second chapter. The rationale for this is the bald fact that local government systems in each country differ from one another and England represents the bulk of the population covered by local authorities in Britain today, with 376 councils (plus the counties) in England and Wales compared to 58 in Scotland and Northern Ireland. Aside from the examples given, the reader should assume the book is referring to local government in England and Wales. Where any variance exists following the creation of the Welsh Assembly and its role in relation to local government in Wales, this is mentioned.

Writing on this subject always runs the risk of dating quickly. This second edition was published on a timetable that involved a delayed White Paper and an extended review into local government finance and functions. Where possible it has tried to keep in step with developments, but only where these are concrete and finalised rather than proposed or just debated (except in those sections covering frameworks for such discussions). As such, its publication has been determined by sales of the first edition rather than any government timetable. Another triumph for market forces, it would appear.

I would like to thank Mark Sandford, John Houghton and Robert Shaw for their suggestions on various early drafts, and also the Council of Local Authorities for International Relations for their co-operation in allowing me to bring this second edition to fruition.

1   Historical development

History of the development of English local councils, from feudal origins to the Victorian golden age, municipal enterprise, Thatcherite reform and Blairite consolidation; with brief notes on Scottish, Welsh and Northern Irish development.

Before 1835

Local government in the United Kingdom is a settled feature of the constitutional architecture and has long acted as an agency of the state in order to fulfil many of the functions required by central government to ameliorate social problems throughout the years. The evolution of local government represents a journey through British social history in the nineteenth and twentieth centuries and its function and nature represent this as such.

The need for a comprehensive system of local authorities arose alongside the expansion in the population of urban centres around the time of the Industrial Revolution, with the old administrative units of what constituted a 'local state' unable to cope with the demands placed on them, such as disease, sanitation problems, squalor and unemployment. But until this juncture, the local state had survived in its compact and limited form of feudal administrative and judicial governance under the 'squirearchy' of the local magistracy in the rural shire counties and the unelected corporations of aldermen (a Saxon term, i.e. 'elder men') in the boroughs.

The theory of the state that prevailed during this period dictated that if there were sufficient means for the collection of taxes to fund the 'defence of the realm', keep the 'King's peace' and maintain the 'King's highways', then there was little need for any degree of elected government beyond that at the local level. In fact, statecraft remained in its infancy and the limited forms of local governance existing were based on expediency rather than any kind of political need, this being the age of the *Curia Regis*, where the monarch and his advisers ruled by edict and where the 'liberties of the subject' entailed a small state and the freedom to do anything the law didn't forbid. As such, local custom and circumstance could be as binding as statute. In a largely rural and agrarian society this theory held sway for many years, with the small enfranchised populations of large urban centres, known as 'boroughs', electing their members of Parliament alongside those in the rural shires, known as 'counties'.

Indeed, until very recently the notion of 'small government' was the preferred 'British' norm and it remains venerated by some. Like the features of the French system of government, such as *gendarmes* and prefects, many of the ancient local institutions and office holders of English local government survive to this day, if in name only. Though the hundred as an administrative division, introduced by the Saxons, has disappeared since the wane of the manorial system, the shire remains in use today. In Yorkshire, the three shire counties were actually known as 'ridings' (North, East and West), which was a Norse term meaning 'third' derived from its Viking heritage (its hundreds were instead known as 'wapentakes').

To understand the role and nature of local government during this feudal era, some consideration should be given to how the administrative units worked in the shire counties and the urban boroughs. These local councils were, ostensibly, local electoral colleges for the selection of Members of Parliament. On several occasions, monarchs had tried to interfere with the local authorities in order to control the membership of Parliament. The Test Acts and the Corporation Act 1661 restricted membership in the boroughs to members of the Church of England. James II granted new charters to some boroughs that narrowed the franchise for elected MPs. Local authorities existed in a very real legal sense, but they were not the only units of government. In many cases, voluntary associations and commercial concerns would exercise some of the roles required to manage the local administration of a range of duties such as poor relief and the stewardship of common lands. Eventually this diverse range of local bodies became more coherently organised along the lines of the parishes, boroughs and counties that would be familiar to most today. Generally the parish was responsible for administrating law and order within its boundaries by appointing a constable, providing common amenities and administering poor relief through the overseers of the poor. The basis for choosing these figures varied from locality to locality, some being elected and others being appointed.

The townships (boroughs) that had obtained a royal charter granting them local privileges, for example, the right to own corporate property such as town halls or refer to themselves as a 'city', were able to regulate the affairs of their inhabitants through the collection of local taxes and the appointment of a 'bench' of magistrates, and furthermore elect members of Parliament (hence the prevailing usage of the term 'Rotten Boroughs' in the case of those that had ceased to be populated). The system of letters patent by the monarch granting city status to a town was usually reserved for towns acting as an established regional base for the Church of England with a longstanding cathedral sited within its boundaries. The number of cities has increased over time, with many conurbations now possessing city status. Cities such as Ripon and Ely have been swallowed up by larger local authorities situated around them, by virtue of their small size, which makes them unviable as a separate local authority solely for the purposes of preserving a city.

In addition to the borough corporations, in many localities associations of craftsmen and merchants came together in 'gilds' (or guilds). These bodies complemented the chartered corporation and for regulating local trade and commercial affairs, they were able to benefit from involvement in civic life. In fact, many practices of the guilds, such as the election of officials, providing representation and accountability to their members, eventually found their way into local government. In some towns, the guild was so important that the guildhall also served as the town hall and some still do so to this day.

This system remains in place as the means by which the sitting councillors of the corporation are elected in the City of London (the famous 'square mile' containing the financial district), where members of ancient livery companies and aldermen still play an active role in the governance of part of a major world city. Despite pressure to modernise the franchise, the corporation remains committed to the system and has resisted pressure to reform the franchise by simply allowing businesses to vote.

Crown-appointed justices of the peace, who had the right to inspect the administration of other local bodies, maintain order and punish petty crime, oversaw the running of the counties. Furthermore, they were responsible for the maintenance of highways and bridges. In addition to these were the numerous bodies such as turnpike trusts and improvement commissions (in a way, the forerunners of today's quangos), who, acting as statutory bodies in some areas, were also responsible for highways, as well as for water and sanitation. Many of these functions required individual Acts of Parliament to sanction the creation of a local body. It is estimated that individual towns established hundreds of paving commissioners and improvement commissioners but Acts of Parliament established 1,114 turnpike trusts, 125 boards of guardians for the poor and several hundred drainage boards. These institutions arose by accident rather than by design over the course of time and as such began to strain under the sufferance of roles that they were not originally expected to carry out.

The 1835 Municipal Corporations Act

As we have seen, industrial society developed at a rapid rate and the system of limited unelected government by the counties and boroughs was deemed to be obsolete and incapable of dealing with the demands placed upon it. The liberal and social reformers of the day were becoming increasingly vocal in calling for a new system of comprehensive local administration that was suitably equipped to deal with the attendant social issues that the new age brought with it.

We can trace the birth of municipalised local democracy back to 1835. The Royal Commission to Inquire into the Municipal Corporations was brought into existence by virtue of the widely felt perception that the municipal corporations, such as they were, had fallen into a state of major malaise and that reform was very much overdue and necessary.

During this period, the corollary of local authorities' actions had

5

a wider impact in other areas of our constitution and affected the quality of life for everyone. The commission was packed with, as Sidney and Beatrice Webb later referred to them, 'eager young intellectuals of Whig opinions'. This was deliberate, to ensure that the commission reported back with radical proposals for reform. It found that the patchwork of local authorities in existence was archaic, inefficient and inadequate and the process of reform was then begun, culminating in the Municipal Corporations Act 1835, which sought to tidy up the arrangements for local government at large and ensure that members of local councils were directly elected. However, when implemented, vast sections of the local populace were in fact automatically disenfranchised when parish overseers neglected to include the cottages of the poor in the rate books. In effect, the franchise for the selection of local representatives was as narrow as before. As a result, the 178 boroughs found themselves tied to strict spending limits through their smaller rates income (it was not until 1948 with the Representation of the People Act that the franchise for local elections was widened to include non-ratepayers such as the wives and adult dependants of the actual ratepayer in the house). With stricter rules regarding funding and audits, councils found themselves being forced to become very cautious about spending. Legal decisions had the effect of making local authorities accountable for every penny they spent and out-lawed spending outside their designated function, measures that had been virtually unknown under the previous system.

The former local authorities had come to be renowned for their financial extravagance and irresponsibility. The elections of 1836 had the effect of bringing new blood into the town halls and ushering in a new breed of local councillor (the City of London was left alone by the legislation). The former inhabitants of nearly all council chambers had been predominantly Tory and Church of

England but direct elections saw the rise of the Whig nonconformist merchant classes, who took their responsibility to ensure the careful stewardship of the rate fund very seriously.

Furthermore, local authorities themselves lost some of their former core residual functions to newly created specialist bodies. In 1834 the parishes lost their responsibility for local welfare under the Poor Law Amendment Act, which created new elected boards of guardians, based on 'unions' of parishes. The inability of some parishes to maintain law and order led to the creation of borough police forces (closely modelled on the Metropolitan Police) in 1835 and county equivalents in 1839. In some areas, radicals made gains in the local elections, only to be followed by a Tory revival. As such, the stock of the local party machine rose and national party organisations began to take local elections more seriously, as the development of political parties as organisations continued apace and party loyalties hardened during the debates about the extension of the franchise. By the 1900s, local elections were seen as a useful barometer for the estimation in which voters held national parties (an electoral behaviour pattern that persists to this day).

A landmark piece of legislation in the development of English local government, the Municipal Corporations Act 1835 was a direct result of the inquiry into the state of English local government, which had reported back with negative conclusions. The Act followed the Reform Act 1832, which had the effect of extending the franchise on a limited basis to more of the middle classes.

However, the inquiry found that despite extending the franchise at the national level, locally many boroughs were corrupt and poorly run and some, such as the oft-cited Old Sarum, had descended into the state of having an MP but no voters on the electoral roll whatsoever. The Municipal Corporations Act was the first in a series of catch-all Acts to apply best practices across all of England's 178 boroughs and included the provision of representative government, an extended franchise, administrative efficiency and financial probity standards. These best practices were gleaned from what were at the time regarded as 'go-ahead' corporations.

The urbanisation of Britain prompted the decline of rural local government. Whereas towns had governed a smaller percentage of the national population in previous times, the clamour to live near the new sources of employment around the burgeoning manu-facturing and engineering industries of the towns caused a decline in the rural population and hence in rural politics. The local govern-ment of rural communities was far from democratic, based as it was on the political norms and values of the landed gentry. However, reform in this area stalled for many years for the following reasons. The impetus to reform county government was not as acute as that in the cities and the towns, where corruption and financial extra-vagance had become commonplace. The main obstacle, however, was the salient fact that Parliament was dominated by rural interests, who saw no need to threaten their own local power bases and political baronies.

Similar to the preceding era, the progress of local government transpired through local variation and circumstance. The 1840s saw local councils obtain greater powers through the provision of local Acts of Parliament – council-sponsored Bills enacted by the Westminster Parliament for the needs and circumstances of a particular locality. The drawback of this mechanism was that if a local authority was successful in petitioning Parliament for a Bill to provide, say, a new bridge, another Bill would be required subse-quently to demolish it. However, during this era, many councils across England sought to advance the cause of local improvement – securing legislative change to make specific provision for their local area. For instance, in 1846, both Newcastle-upon-Tyne and Burnley boroughs sought to prohibit the building of new houses that did not have privies attached to them, while Chester and Leicester acquired the right to construct public gardens and recreation grounds.

These local legislative experiments had knock-on effects for national legislation – the original laws governing the treatment of, and prohibiting cruelty towards, animals originated from local Acts in the Midlands. As was the spirit of the Victorian age, many councils sought powers to regulate public morals – Liverpool led the way in regulating the pawnbrokers' trade whereas Leeds acquired powers to control brothels. Birmingham sought new powers for its local police force, beyond what were operating in other local authorities during that era. In what could be seen as the beginnings of civic rivalry, many councils copied the Acts of other councils or sought to go beyond them with their own. Nationally, this era of improvement was consolidated upon by a series of Acts that sought to take the best practices of individual local authorities and apply them to all the municipal corporations through national generic local government legislation.

In spite of the reforms, the problems associated with the industrial age were increasing in their prevalence, rather than diminishing. The diseases normally associated with this era – cholera, tuberculosis etc. – could not be contained by local authorities under their designated function, with most towns not possessing sufficient sewerage or water treatment facilities. In this regard, the Public Health Act 1848 is a landmark in the history of local government. It was a consolidation of the best provisions of local Acts in this area and gave councils the power to enact sufficient measures in order to try to contain the spread of disease through their burgeoning populations. However, the scope of the Act was limited in so far as it did not apply across the whole country but only where the General Board of Health thought it should or where individual local authorities had adopted it.

Despite the best intentions of the reformers in Parliament, and for all its own intentions of evolving alongside the urbanisation of the nation, local government remained in a state of chaos. The unsophisticated nature of local politics, developed in a vacuum without the benefit of the Westminster experience, was reduced to an unedifying farce in many councils with petty rivalries and squabbles taking precedence over the needs of local citizens. Thus the attentions of national reformers turned to containing local democracy in an attempt to render it more effective.

The public health movement

If someone was to sit down and design a system of local government from scratch, even in the nineteenth century it would beggar belief that anyone could have found the British system to be adequate for the needs of an emerging modern society. From 1835 onwards, the history of British local government became a legislative one. The patchwork of British local government in the nineteenth century, as we have noted, evolved alongside British society as urbanisation continued apace. Throughout this period, on top of the plethora of commissioners and local bodies already in place, we can add library commissioners, commissioners of baths and washhouses, burial boards and inspectors of lighting and watching as new purposeful local bodies that sprang up according to the demands of society.

However, the considerable health disorders and sanitation problems that blighted urban life still continued to prove an insurmountable challenge for parish-centred British local government and its antiquated workings. Although the call for reform was made as early as 1836 with Joseph Hume's County Board Bill, change was actively sought by what was termed the 'public health movement', led by the Benthamite Liberal Edwin Chadwick. The 1868 Royal Sanitary

Commission heard many pleas for action on drainage and sanitation in English towns up and down the country. The lack of central control and direction was mentioned several times during the commission's existence. However, both local and central government resisted centralisation. Its advocates relied upon the evidence of widespread poverty and squalor in the towns and cities and the ineffectual nature of local authorities to deal with the problems that manifested themselves through poor drainage and sanitation. Those against cited England's tradition of local custom and circumstance as the guiding hand in local affairs.

Following the report of the Royal Commission in 1871, centralisation came, albeit belatedly and ineffectually, through the setting up of the Local Government Board as part of the civil service in that year. The intention of this move towards some degree of centralised control of local government affairs was an attempt to provide some national standards for local services, the reform of local government until this point being reliant upon MPs sponsoring Bills in Parliament to consolidate observed best local practice. However, local governance in the counties had escaped scrutiny and reform until this juncture, with county government acting as the last bulwark of the squirearchy and the political power base of the aristocracy outside London.

The peculiarities of the boroughs merely extended to the appointment of aldermen – robed former (or aspiring) councillors who were able to sit for terms of six years. County government, on the other hand, was based on the premise that government by unelected magistrates was an acceptable way to do business. Despite the progress made by urban boroughs, rural local government was widely held to be lagging behind, with all the attendant social problems and issues this brought. In Parliament, rural reform of county government was a battleground between urban radicals and the representatives of the squirearchy, who still held sway and who were reluctant to countenance any reforms drawn up by the radicals who could yet control any elected local council. County government was still based on magistrates meeting in quarter sessions, although an earlier Royal Commission had in 1835 recommended that county ratepayers should have some say in how their rates were spent, albeit through elected councillors sitting alongside ex-officio magistrates. Reform, however, was delayed by half a century by virtue of the powerful rural lobby in Parliament.

Following the passage of the Representation of the People Act 1884 (the 'Third Reform Bill') and the enfranchisement of a greater number of working men, moves towards the creation of a wholly elected county tier of local government took legislative shape in 1886 when the Liberal government attempted to promote a Bill in Parliament that was closely modelled on the Municipal Corporations Act 1835. Similarly, the Conservatives, divided on the issue in Parliament thanks to its large rural lobby, promoted a Bill to this end in 1888, which eventually became the Local Government Act 1888; like the 1835 Act, a landmark in local government history as it brought into being the two-tier system of counties and boroughs or districts that still exists in most areas to this day. However, for the Bill to pass, several amendments had to be inserted as concessions to its detractors. Early hints of radical devolutionary measures from central government to the new county councils were removed altogether from the Bill. In order to prevent overlapping jurisdictions or force urban and rural representatives to have to sit together in the council chamber (or to have to pay for each other's services), a number of county boroughs (unitary boroughs outside county jurisdiction) were created in order to reflect urban/rural geography.

However, by virtue of amendments tabled to the Bill, the number of these county boroughs increased significantly in order to offend as few people as possible and for all manner of peculiar local circumstances, not least ecclesiastical concerns. So a situation arose where a small county such as Rutland could have the same level of governance as a large Yorkshire riding. Another facet of the original Bill, a proposal to reorder the smaller local authorities, was also dropped. However, this became a separate Act under the subsequent Liberal government, the Local Government Act 1894, which had the effect of rationalising the plethora of boards etc., and creating new urban and rural district councils to replace them. It also gave explicit legal recognition in government to parish councils as a community-based tier of small-scale local governance. By 1899, local government in England had become a multi-tiered system reflecting differing local circumstances but substantially more rationalised than in 1834.

Pressure to respect local civic identities had been applied in Parliament in order to halt the number of proposed county boroughs so as to protect some of the boroughs not considered capable of exercising this role. Therefore the qualifying population level for each borough to attain county borough status, allowing them to be exempt from the jurisdiction of the new county councils, which became 'live' local authorities in 1889, was raised to 50,000.

One new county council that became live in 1889 was London County Council (LCC), frequently held up as an example of municipal socialism in action. Municipal socialism first became evident in the programme of the radical Liberal Joseph Chamberlain, who as leader of Birmingham municipalised the city's gas company in 1875 and its water supply in 1876. The leading Labour thinker G. D. H. Cole was later led to remark that the ideas of municipal socialism were 'based more than most Fabians cared to acknowledge on Joseph Chamberlain's'.

A coalition of Liberals and Fabians (a founding body of the Labour Party), known as Progressives, took power following the council's inaugural elections in 1889, winning 70 of the 118 seats, and began the municipalisation of London's services, including the provision of public housing, a radical measure for the time. The LCC followed the boundaries of the Metropolitan Board of Works (created following the 'Great Stink' on the Thames) to provide sewerage in and around the City of London, and had been carved out of areas of Middlesex, Surrey and Kent. Members of the ruling group included Sidney Webb (who became chairman of the Technical Instruction Committee) and Will Crooks (chairman of the Public Control Committee), who would both go on to become prominent Labour Party figures. This managed to frighten the Conservatives, who in 1899 made provision for another Local Government Act, which had the effect of creating twenty-eight independent borough councils in an attempt to restrain the influence of the Progressive-dominated LCC. The gesture ultimately backfired as many of the boroughs, such as Woolwich and Poplar, fell to the control of working-class councillors. Under the direction of Fabians such as Webb, the LCC fulfilled a municipal socialist vision of its services being run for the common good of the people, as outlined in his London Programme in the 1890s. This sought the collective monopoly provision of municipalised local services in areas such as gas, water, docks, markets, trams, hospitals and housing. Through several Acts of Parliament the LCC became responsible for drainage, the fire service, controls on building and, in conjunction with the boroughs, public housing. Its municipal enterprise extended to buying out all the London tram companies, doubling the provision of parks and digging two road tunnels under the Thames. In existence between 1889 and 1965 (when it was replaced by the short-lived Greater London Council), it was dominated by the Progressives from 1889 to 1907, the Conservatives from 1907 to 1934 and Labour from 1934 to 1965, and in particular it was notable for its extensive provision of hospital services and social housing, as has been noted. This came at the end of the incremental constitutional revolution in local government that was the nineteenth century.

However, while the ensuing period of local government history could be regarded as stable in terms of reforms driven from the centre, it was most notable for the tension between local and central government and the role of local politics in the formation of the nascent Labour Party through its control of boroughs such as Poplar, East Ham and Woolwich during the early twentieth century.

Early twentieth century

Despite minor fits of experimentation previously, by the turn of the twentieth century local councils remained perfunctory bodies concerned with the daily supervision of sanitation, drainage and highways. This notwithstanding, the state of English local government was in a tidier state than a hundred years previously, when the incoherent muddle that served as local government was unelected and completely lacking in co-ordination.

The elections to school boards and boards of guardians had become politically charged, whereas in the mid-nineteenth century they were merely seen as the outlet for the civic-mindedness of the middle classes. In 1902, education became the responsibility of local authorities (poor relief passing to them in 1929). The late nineteenth and early twentieth century was notable for the advances in mental health provision, with clear local authority duties superseding the anarchic and inhumane provision for the mentally ill in the Victorian era. Furthermore, the activities of municipal socialists had not passed unnoticed and the Liberty and Property Defence League sprang up to act as a bulwark against what was seen as an assault on private property by pioneering socialist councils.

However, it was Parliament and the judiciary that were able to assuage the concerns of the liberty-conscious citizens, ruling in many instances that local authorities were acting ultra vires in their endeavours. Some councils 'massaged' previous legislation such as the Artisans and Labourers' Dwellings Act 1868 and the Housing Act 1890 to justify their house-building policies.

By 1945, local government was effectively politicised, with clear partisan groupings based on party political lines and whips in the council chambers of most local authorities, whereas in the nineteenth century, the ethos of non-political public service had characterised the dealings of most councillors. The nineteenth century was characterised by the Tory–Whig, later Conservative–Liberal, duopolies in the party system, although towards the end of the century the nascent municipal socialist groupings had begun to spring up in some urban councils. Along with the Progressive coalition in London, there were independent groupings on many councils and certainly ratepayers on most. Many cities and towns gàve birth to short-lived local civic groupings such as the Bristol Citizens Party and the Southampton Independent Party. In London, the Conservatives organised on the LCC under the quaint epithet of the London Municipal Society, whereas in Bradford the left went under the banner of the Bradford Workers' Municipal Federation. Throughout the twentieth century it is possible to find many local and bizarre examples of the small party on the council – with defections from the main parties by disgruntled party group members giving rise to all manner of short-lived local political endeavours.

The local elections in 1919 saw a low turnout but huge advances for Labour in urban England, including taking control of a significant number of London boroughs and English cities and becoming serious power brokers in others. The electoral advances of the Labour Party mirrored the decline of the Liberal Party nationally and the 'red scare' rhetoric of the Zinoviev letter was copied locally as civic-minded Conservatives sought to halt the encroaching advance of local socialism. Consequently, the local elections of 1922 saw Labour lose many of its recently gained council seats, such as in Hackney, where, having taken control of the council in 1919, Labour lost all its seats (including Herbert Morrison's). The ideological debate within the Labour Party was concerned with what role local councils should play in terms of improving the lives of their citizens.

Before he became the seventh leader of the Labour Party, George Lansbury shot to prominence as the radical leader of Poplar Borough Council in east London in the 1920s. The borough of Poplar was noted for its municipal socialist zeal, building washhouses, libraries, parks and swimming baths. In 1921 Poplar under Lansbury defied the coalition government of Lloyd George over the operation of the Poor Law benefits by refusing to pay its precept to the LCC, resulting in the imprisonment of thirty councillors and giving rise to the term 'Poplarism'. It is reputed that sympathetic crowds visited the jails at Holloway and Brixton and sang 'The Red Flag', and the councillors' defiant attitude to the sovereignty of Parliament was quite clearly present in the title of their pamphlet *Guilty and Proud of It*.

The effects of Poplarism became widespread as more than twenty councils resisted the cuts and refused to implement the unpopular means test for the unemployed. There is no doubt that the actions of Labour-dominated Poor Law guardians in urban Britain eventually led to the repeal of the Poor Law legislation and removing the Dickensian conditions of the workhouse. (Tory health minister Neville Chamberlain was so incensed by the activities of renegade socialist boards of guardians and inept Tory and Liberal ones that he abolished them altogether in 1929.) Some pointed to Poplarism as a means to confront the legitimacy of central government whereas others advocated the Fabian approach of gradually building up the size of the local public sector by stealth. Certainly the Labour Party's establishment at national level viewed Poplarism with nothing but disdain, conscious as ever of the need to be perceived as moderate and respectful for the rule of law.

As has been previously stated, this era was certainly notable for its approach to experimenting with municipal social ownership – some Labour local authorities decided to try their hand at providing health centres, electricity provision and municipal savings banks. Councils also discovered the ability to regulate the working lives of local people through contract compliance, where councils stipulated the hours, wages and union rights of employees working for private firms that bid for council contracts. In 1923, Poplar Council made illegal payments in unemployment benefit to dockers in the London dock strikes of that year. The boroughs of Battersea, Bermondsey, Bethnal Green, Poplar and Woolwich refused to reduce council workers' wages, against the wishes of Whitehall.

The Housing and Town Planning Act 1919 enabled local authorities to build more social housing and in Labour areas this was set upon with much aplomb. The late 1920s saw Labour retake many of its earlier losses as it gained control of towns and cities once again, particularly in Yorkshire. It is at this point where we can see how local elections became a political barometer for central government, although it wasn't until 1945 that Labour saw local successes translate into a breakthrough in the national polls. The economic depression in the early 1930s placed a strain on local authorities through the extra demand for poor relief and again this saw a rise in municipal militancy, although the Poor Law system was already facing abolition. The Unemployment Assistance Board set up in 1934 was to some extent the first stage of removing local authorities from the welfare state.

The 1930s are quite often remembered for the ideological excesses of the age, poverty and increasing international instability, leading some political activists to flirt with communism and even fascism in a minority of cases. The British Union of Fascists (BUF) contested the 1937 LCC elections, obtaining small pockets of notable support in areas such as Bethnal Green (the notorious Nazi sympathiser William Joyce, better known as Lord Haw-Haw, in fact stood as a BUF candidate). However, it was the Communists who obtained electoral success in the East End that year in Stepney, while the borough of Finsbury was quickly dubbed the 'People's Republic of Finsbury' for its erection of a statue of Lenin. There can be no doubt that the actions of Labour local authorities during this time did much to ameliorate the bleak and harsh conditions faced by the urban poor and went some way towards attracting more supporters to the party, this manifesting itself in the local elections of 1937.

The Conservatives dominated the LCC between 1907 and 1934 and although radicalism and innovation were largely left to the boroughs, they did embark upon an extensive building programme of housing estates in outlying areas of south London (arguably this dispersed the working classes out of the inner-city areas and therefore had the unwitting effect of placing them into hitherto safe suburban Tory parliamentary seats, to their cost in 1945). The building of social housing was accelerated during this period, as councils sought to diminish the Victorian-era urban squalor that still existed in many areas. Labour also made electoral breakthroughs in cities such as Norwich and Lincoln and retook the LCC in 1934.

The LCC in the pre-war era is synonymous with Herbert Morrison, who, although serving as Minister for Transport in the 1929–31 Labour government, also found time to be a local government leader as well as a parliamentarian. Beatrice Webb remarked: 'He is a Fabian of Fabians; a direct disciple of Sidney Webb's . . . the very quintessence of Fabianism in policy and outlook.' The LCC deservedly obtained a reputation for being well run (Morrison was obsessed with efficiency and ethical conduct) and in 1937 Morrison's Labour Party was re-elected and increased its number of seats on a high turnout.

Post-war planning and consensus

The Labour government elected in 1945 was in fact notable for the inclusion of three former councillors amongst its senior Cabinet members (Clement Attlee, Herbert Morrison and Aneurin Bevan). During the vast expansion of the post-war welfare state, local government was the unsung hero as central government, under the auspices of the first Labour government to serve a full term with a large parliamentary majority, sought to bring about a Keynesian economy and gave life to William Beveridge's social policy. Written in 1942 when victory over the Axis powers was far from assured, the Beveridge report promised a vision of society far removed from the harsh reality of pre-war Britain, where the 'five giants' of want, squalor, disease, ignorance and idleness, which the report was intended to fight, were commonplace during the 1920s and 1930s.

Ushering in an era of consensus-led politics, local government was to become a key agency for service provision in social democratic Britain. Furthermore, the regeneration required in the inner cities after the German bombing of the Second World War saw local authorities in a pivotal role, although the need for a quick recovery and the experience of government by regional commissioners during the war recast the perception of local authorities and their capacity to deliver on national priorities.

Despite Labour's grandiose visions for the National Health Service, which eventually came to fruition in 1948, it was originally anticipated that universal healthcare would be a function of local authorities, which already administered a large number of hospitals. However, Bevan was convinced that a National Health Service should be run by central government through regional agencies and therefore the remaining local authority and voluntary sector hospitals would have to be brought into the fold. Centralisation also continued apace under the nationalisation of transport, with the Transport Act 1947 transferring canals and harbours to the new British Transport Commission and the River Boards Act 1948 creating new bodies to supervise waterway anti-pollution. Britain's new motorways, a hallmark of optimism of that era, were built under the Special Roads Act 1949, which saw central government responsible for their construction. This mirrored the centralisation under the Trunk Roads Act 1946 (and indeed in 1936 under a similar act) when central government assumed the responsibility to provide new major roads rather than entrust this to local councils.

However, reform of the local franchise (local elections were previously the preserve of ratepayers, not all adults as in parliamentary elections) saw Labour repeat its 1945 general election showing as it took a healthy number of urban areas into its control. Labour's local socialist measures (municipalisation) were being carried out on the national stage (nationalisation), which saw the transfer of local functions such as gas and electricity supply to the boards of nationalised industries. Instead, local government saw its role develop as the provider of state education and social housing, with social services becoming more prominent as a local responsibility in the 1960s. However, while Bevan did his level best to remove local authorities' responsibilities in the sphere of health provision, he did introduce legislation that allowed them not only to regulate aspects of local leisure activities but also to play a leading part in their provision, especially cultural activities such as museums.

The seemingly ceaseless flow of local government reform proposals (there was another Royal Commission sitting from 1923 to 1929) was temporarily halted during the war, but upon the resumption of government as usual in 1945 a five-man commission was appointed to 'consider the boundaries of the local government areas in England and Wales (except London) and related questions such as the establishment of new county boroughs'. The commission was fairly critical of the local government system as it stood and recommended an overhaul of the counties and boroughs to meet the government's aim of 'individually and collectively effective and convenient units of local government administration'.

The 1945–51 Labour governments were regarded as economically and socially radical, but they were not known for their reforming zeal in the arena of the constitution and despite their best intentions at the start, it is not surprising that local government reform was rejected and the commission stood down. For all the advances made with the Education Act 1944, Labour acted somewhat cautiously on education reform once in government, refusing to cave in to grassroots and intellectual pressure to introduce comprehensive schooling. Education minister Ellen Wilkinson, generally regarded as a doyenne of the left, actually favoured the retention of grammar schools as a means of creating a 'working-class elite'. Meanwhile, the social experiment that was the New Towns was based on cultivating model communities in place of the squalor previously known by Labour supporters, although those chosen to populate them had to be respectable model families themselves.

In 1946 the National Assistance Act was introduced, a landmark piece of legislation in so far as it obliged councils to undertake some form of social services and abolished the Poor Law, which had been in place since 1601. However, one of the most striking political dividing lines between Labour and the Conservatives locally during this period was the level of council rents. Labour's local socialism ensured that rents were kept low for the working classes whereas the Conservatives sought to keep rents at market levels. The Rent Act 1957 even resulted in riots in north London when Conservative-controlled St Pancras Borough Council raised its rents in 1960. Social housing became an important element of Labour's 'Homes fit for heroes' rhetoric after the war, with the house-building programmes initiated under this far exceeding the programmes of the more radical and ambitious councils before the war. This agenda was shared by the Conservatives, who upon taking power in 1951 continued the programme of demolishing pre-war slums and bombed-out areas in the inner cities and replacing them with more modern living spaces. It should be noted, however, that the preference here was for private provision and that standards in public programmes were not as high, which, for instance, used high-rise tower blocks of flats to house large numbers of slum dwellers; these blocks would themselves become 'slums on stilts' over time and present another generation with an issue to address.

The appetite for local government reform did not remain sated for long during the post-war period and inevitably the Conservative government of Harold Macmillan, which boasted that it had built more homes than the erstwhile Labour government, established two new Local Government Commissions in 1958, one for England and one for Wales, their lifetimes continuing into the Labour government of Harold Wilson in 1964.

The English commission utilised a novel approach for its

examinations of the many local councils that it surveyed, in that the commission examined five 'Special Review Areas', based in the provinces outside London, in which it could set the boundary status of the counties, and could then examine and review the districts beneath them. As can be imagined, this led to a cumbersome process, and the opportunities for vested interests to delay reform under this system were many. The recommendations of the commission for Wales were rejected altogether and the English commission was wound up in 1965, when the Labour government decided to create another Royal Commission to undertake a more detailed analysis with firmer terms of reference.

Furthermore, the issue of London governance remained pressing for a national government ensconced in the capital and keenly aware of its activities, although individual MPs representing seats outside London would of course be aware of what was going on in their own local authorities.

By the late 1950s it was widely acknowledged that London had outgrown its nineteenth-century local government institutions. Yet another Royal Commission was appointed in 1957 to look at ways of providing a tier of local government that covered the greater London region rather than just the inner London area that fell under the LCC's jurisdiction. It should be noted that the LCC was, before and after the war, ostensibly a Labour institution and a successful one at that. The commission unanimously recommended the creation of a Greater London Council (GLC), taking in Conservative areas in Surrey and Kent (as was the government's intention) as well as the Essex areas of the Thames corridor, a small area of Hertfordshire and almost the entire county of Middlesex, with as many powers as possible passing to the boroughs beneath it. The recommendations were acted upon in the London Government Act 1963, although the government did amend the size of the proposed authority. Upon its creation, the GLC followed the pattern of Labour administration as per the LCC in the inaugural elections of 1964, though at the second set of elections, three years later, the Conservatives took control of London's government for the first time in a generation, holding on in 1970 also. Labour returned to power at County Hall in 1973 following unpopular service cuts, only to lose again four years later (the term of office was extended to four years in 1972 alongside the abolition of aldermen). See also 'Note: London' below.

Politically this period was often noted for its adherence to the 'social-democratic consensus' and local government, aside from a few minor skirmishes between the parties, was no exception. However, while both main parties in Parliament agreed that local government could not continue to operate on the lines which it had for over a century, neither of them actually managed to grasp the nettle of reform to a degree that displayed any real results in terms of overhauling the structure. In any case, there had been piecemeal reform as a continual process since the creation of county councils in 1889, and the presence in Parliament of those who considered 'bread and butter issues' to be of far greater relevance ensured that reform would have to wait, almost until the end of the period of consensus itself.

Throughout the 1960s, the 'social-democratic consensus' remained firmly in place and the period 1964–1979 was dominated by Labour government under Harold Wilson and James Callaghan, save for the electorate's brief flirtation with Edward Heath's 'wet' Conservative government between 1970 and 1974. As we have seen, the issue of municipal reform had not disappeared and the Conservatives' attempts at reform had yielded nothing.

During the post-war period local government remained held in high regard by the main political parties at Westminster, viewed as an essential agency for the provision of services on the ground. However, as the cracks began to appear in the national social-democratic consensus, it found its friends dwindling in number for one reason or another. In an era in which political scandal was becoming more commonplace (mirroring the rise of television and the eschewal of deference by Fleet Street), the 'Poulson affair' stands out as one of the more regrettable episodes in the Labour Party's history and certainly as the most salient example of corruption in local government during recent times. The Poulson affair derives its name from the (unqualified) architect John Poulson, who was involved in a number of mediocre municipal architecture commissions in the 1960s and 1970s, although none more famous than the work he undertook for T. Dan Smith's Newcastle. Smith was a charismatic local political leader whose grandiose visions for Newcastle in its era of municipal improvement included turning it into a regional power base ('the Brasilia of the north') for a devolved north-eastern government, even going so far as to build space for 124 elected members of a putative north-eastern regional assembly in its council chamber. Smith became a lobbyist for, and eventual business partner of, Poulson and sought to convince other council leaders to commission him as an architect for their own municipal building programmes, relying on corrupt practices and Masonic networks to further this. When Poulson filed for bankruptcy in 1972, Smith's 'crony' network was brought down with him. The episode left a bitter taste in Labour's mouth for some time to come and certainly dented the credibility, in the minds of a few, of local government's ability to manage the stewardship of resources honestly.

During the thirteen years between 1951 and 1964 that Labour was in opposition at Westminster, the demand for the introduction of comprehensive secondary schools as a means to abolish selective education had gone from being a lofty egalitarian ideal to actual party policy. Grassroots opinion amongst Labour Party activists, and indeed many councillors, was frustrated at the lack of education reform under the Labour governments of 1945–51, especially in the area of comprehensive schooling.

A small number of local authorities (such as the LCC) did, however, proceed along the comprehensive route of schooling before Anthony Crosland as Secretary of State for Education issued Circular 10/65, which had the effect of requesting that local education authorities (LEAs) consider moving their schools over to the comprehensive system (although his junior minister Reg Prentice, a future defector to the Tories, favoured a more mandatory approach). This approach was seen as more likely to deliver – the imposition of comprehensive schooling from the centre would be fiercely resisted by many local authorities, especially the Tory shires. The plans faltered in many areas as Labour suffered huge losses to the Conservatives in 1968 in many councils, the Tories being vehemently in favour of the retention of grammar schools.

Upon assuming her post as Conservative Secretary of State for Education, Margaret Thatcher immediately rescinded Circular 10/65 but the policy was revived once Prentice became Labour education secretary in 1974, and his 1976 Education Act was specifically enacted to deal with those LEAs that refused to countenance comprehensive education. It was, of course, rescinded in 1979 when the Conservatives took office once again. However, this merely served to stem the tide of grammar school conversions to comprehensives, as selective schools were now the exception rather than the rule in most areas of the country.

We have noted the Conservative governments of 1951–1964 and their attempts to reform the boundaries and structures of local government. The issue was revived and given extra political weight under the Royal Commissions set up by Richard Crossman as Minister for Housing and Local Government in 1966 – the Redcliffe-Maud Commission in England and Wales (which included T. Dan Smith) and the Wheatley Commission in Scotland. The commissions were given clearer terms of reference and left alone to examine the workings of the local government system, which was by now widely felt to be antiquated and of little political relevance as a result, although one could consider the commissions' work in the context of the Wilsonian drive for modernisation at the time. The Redcliffe-Maud Commission found a number of deficiencies in the way local authorities did their business, for example:

- the boundaries of most local authorities did not correspond to those of notional communities and local identities as many urban areas had grown beyond local authority boundaries;
- the scale of fragmentation of local authority jurisdictions;
- the confusion as to which authority did what;
- the size of the smaller authorities and their ability to be effective.

The commission published its report in 1969, which aimed for a more rational division of responsibilities within local government and for boundaries that made more sense to the people it served. The proposals the report came up with were based on the need to reconcile the interests of town and country and 'strike a balance between the claims of efficiency, democracy, community and continuity'.

It recommended that England should be divided into fifty-eight areas of unitary authorities (akin to the status of the county boroughs). Three areas of England (Merseyside, south-east Lancashire/north-east Cheshire and the West Midlands) should have a two-tier system (akin to the new Greater London Council and the London boroughs). The commission also recommended that two other non-operational tiers should be introduced: local councils that could provide a minor representational role and regional councils to provide a strategic planning element to the proceedings. The commission was divided on some questions of geography and one member, Derek Senior, issued a lengthy Memorandum of Dissent which called for a city region framework instead. The city region vogue for urban governance was instead indulged through the creation of the Passenger Transport Authorities under the Passenger Transport Act 1968, which saw the responsibility for public transport in metropolitan areas shifted to joint boards. The commission's main findings received a mixed response, some proposals being more palatable than others, but Harold Wilson's Labour government accepted the report. The election of Edward Heath's Conservative government in 1970 prevented the Labour government from implementing it in any case.

The ranks of Labour councillors are often swelled by elderly party members (an abiding trend to this day) but when many of these lost their seats in the late 1960s, many of them were too old to be re-elected in the 1970s, thus allowing a new intake of councillors to take office. These councillors were quite often left-wing and as such we saw a new era of local authorities challenging the wisdom of central government, regardless of its political complexion. A minor flashpoint of 1970s municipal militancy came in 1972, when Clay Cross Urban District Council in Derbyshire refused to observe the new Housing Finance Act (obliging it to raise its rents) and, following a period of non-co-operation with the demands of central government and the commissioner appointed to temporarily supervise the collection of council rents, the 'Clay Cross Eleven' (as they became known) were disqualified from office.

Aside from housing and the powers to ensure decent standards of hygiene and sanitation, local government was coming under pressure to take an active lead in personal social services on top of its responsibilities under the National Assistance Act 1946. Films such as Ken Loach's *Cathy Come Home* drove this home in terms of raising public awareness. The Local Government Social Services Act 1970 stipulated that local authorities had to create their own social services departments to take the lead in this area in their localities. However, under the National Health Service Act 1973 they lost their remaining responsibilities in terms of local healthcare such as the provision of health centres and ambulances (this was finalised in 1990, when they lost their representation on health authorities altogether).

Many of the reforms proposed by Redcliffe-Maud were predicated on the need to attract a better calibre of councillor to local government. This agenda was furthered by the Bains Committee, a working party set up to advise on management structures in local government to complement the work of Redcliffe-Maud for insertion into the legislation required. The Bains report recommended a streamlined internal management system for the new local authorities and its recommendations were largely accepted by the Heath government as they were less radical than the Redcliffe-Maud proposals and would go some way towards instilling a more 'corporate' approach to the way local authorities did business, as was the managerial approach of the Heath government at the time.

The Redcliffe-Maud report, parked since 1969, made its way into the statute books and town halls across England and Wales, to some extent, in the Local Government Act 1972. The Conservatives had faced internal opposition to the loss of county councils and the government indicated early on that it preferred the evolutionary approach by introducing a comprehensive two-tier system of counties and districts in the majority of England and Wales, and metropolitan counties and metropolitan districts in six urban areas of large population density. The ostensible difference between the two types of county was that functions such as education and social services remained at county level in the shires, whereas in the metropolitan areas they would be carried out by the districts.

The government adopted the 'big is beautiful' approach in terms of counties, preferring large geographical units covering both town and country (the inclusion of rural areas was felt to be of electoral benefit to the Conservatives sitting on county councils). The creation of the three 'artificial' counties of Avon, Cleveland and Humberside was unpopular from the start, although the rural areas included (the source of the opposition) were at the behest of the environment secretary, Peter Walker, in the interests of Tory representation on these largely urban councils. Furthermore, cities such as Bristol, Derby, Leicester and Norwich were reduced to the same status as other (smaller) districts – although they were permitted to retain their conferred 'city' status.

On top of the 1972 reforms, the Local Government Act 1974 created the office of the Local Government Commissioners, more commonly known as 'Ombudsmen', to provide individual redress for local authority misadministration, an overdue measure in terms of providing a greater degree of accountability in the workings of local government. In the spirit of this new era of critically assessing the workings of local government, the Labour government created a Committee of Local Government Finance (the Layfield Committee), which produced its report in 1976. This was the first in a series of attempts to control the growth of local authority expenditure.

Against the backdrop of wider economic uncertainty as the era of Keynesian spending of the social-democratic consensus violently drew to a close (and in furtherance of IMF-imposed spending controls), Anthony Crosland, now Labour environment secretary, was led to remark to an audience of local councillors: 'With its usual spirit of patriotism and its tradition of service to the community's needs, [local government] is coming to realise that, for the time being at least, the party is over.'

Decline and the new urban left

In the late 1970s, the electoral unpopularity of the Labour government of James Callaghan saw the Conservatives take many council seats in urban areas. However, Labour slowly crawled back to power in many councils and the election of Margaret Thatcher in 1979, although setting the scene for a decade of conflict between the tiers of government, represented the high-water mark of Tory success in local government elections.

However, a sea change in local government politics had already taken place, with the ascendant left wing of the Labour Party taking control of many local Labour Parties (and therefore council Labour groups). Sensing betrayal by Harold Wilson and Callaghan, the left's faith in the Parliamentary Labour Party to deliver socialism was considerably dented and an 'extra-parliamentary' strategy was envisaged, with local authorities as one of the frontiers in a pitched battle against the authoritarian state, as in the 1920s with Poplarism. This went beyond the modest ambitions of the 'gas and water socialism' of the early Fabian collectivists. By the time of the 'longest suicide note in history' at the 1983 general election, the term 'loony left' was already being banded around furiously by Fleet Street and the (reported) behaviour of many Labour-controlled local authorities could only add to Labour's electoral woes. Labour local authorities began to see themselves as a bulwark against the individualism and 'greed-is-good' philosophy of Thatcherism. Such an aim could be seen as benign and worthwhile if viewed in this context, although many would argue that it was not something local authorities should have been concerning themselves with.

The agenda of the new urban left in the 1980s deviated from that of its predecessors in the 1920s as it sought to go beyond service provision and became more interested in areas such as equalities, culture and addressing deficits in the national economy, particularly unemployment. The backdrop of increased Cold War anxiety, inner-city riots (particularly the poor community relations profile of the police) and rising unemployment and industrial unrest gave radical Labour local authorities the opportunity to flex their muscles and rattle a few sabres at the Thatcher-led Tory government through gestures such as 'nuclear-free zones'.

If organisations such as the Campaign for Nuclear Disarmament, trade unions such as the National Union of Mineworkers and individuals such as Peter Tatchell exemplified the character of the 'loony left', then Labour local authorities (with one or two exceptions, such as the traditional bastions of Birmingham and Newcastle) proved to be a convenient hangout for the scourges of Fleet Street, Whitehall and probably even the Labour leadership. If one was to believe the more sensationalist scribblings of the tabloid press, then the daily life of an average Labour councillor consisted of thinking up new ways to indoctrinate children into deviant lifestyles and correct linguistic behaviour by banning 'racist' nursery rhymes ('Baa Baa Black Sheep') and 'sexist' terminology ('manholes'). Admittedly Fleet Street hacks were picking on isolated examples of some of the more ridiculous examples of Labour councillors' behaviour, but in some cases the charge was justified when it was argued that many local authorities had become more obsessed with the wider problems of society as they saw them than with merely providing local services.

The advance of the left in the Labour Party was unfortunately associated with the existence of the Trotskyite Militant Tendency, who, although usually lumped in by the media with the likes of the GLC's Ken Livingstone and London borough council leaders of the time such as Linda Bellos and 'Red' Ted Knight, were, politically speaking, actually to the left of most of the new urban left.

The only local authority in which Militant (its name taken from the newspaper enthusiastically sold by its members) exerted any degree of real control was Liverpool, where the Liberals had made some inroads in the 1970s. Alongside 'Red' Ken Livingstone, the women of Greenham Common and miners' leader Arthur Scargill, Liverpool's deputy leader Derek Hatton made a convenient bogeyman for the right-wing press of the time. Liverpool, like many other urban centres during the 1980s, had suffered at the hands of deindustrialisation, with the attendant social problems. Many of its housing estates had fallen into severe neglect and, combined with high levels of unemployment, it was of no surprise that Toxteth took its place alongside Brixton in the inner-city riots of 1981. Liverpool had been Militant's power base outside London since the 1950s and had come to be more influential in the city's Labour Party by the time Labour regained control of the city council from the Liberals in 1983.

The affair was more unfortunate as it came to be associated with the more unsavoury practices of intimidation of opponents, cronyism and a lack of regard for resources. Inevitably, the Labour Party sought to impose control of the city Labour group's affairs and by 1986 the episode was largely over. Indeed, Labour leader Neil Kinnock famously lashed out at Hatton and Co. in his speech to the 1985 Labour Conference. As Hatton left the conference hall in disgust, closely followed by the left-wing firebrand MP Eric Heffer, the high point of municipal militancy was now arguably over, with any flashes of deviation from the approved moderate party line being quelled very quickly by the centre in the battle to make Labour more respectable locally and therefore more electable nationally.

Of course, in any conflict there must be more than one party engaged in the battle and it would not do to leave the Conservative Party out of the analysis. Thatcher's New Right project was disdainful towards the role of local government and the part it played in driving up central government expenditure, and it was a sure-fire target for her intentions to 'roll back' the bloated and over-fed state. But by 1985 the Conservatives in local government were in retreat as councils in places as unlikely as East Sussex and Berkshire were transferred out of their control after almost a century of dominance. In the tradition of Neville Chamberlain's response to Poplarism in the 1920s, Thatcher sought to end central government's reliance on local government as the local agency for the delivery of services.

One of the measures applied by the Conservatives in order to curb excessive town hall spending was rate capping. This saw central government stipulating the maximum rate that could be set by local councils; in many town halls Labour councillors attempted to revolt against the measures by refusing to set a rate in a stand-off against central government. When this was ruled illegal, the number of councils rebelling dropped considerably and by 1985 only Liverpool and Lambeth were left battling, resulting in some councillors being removed from office and surcharged for failing to adhere to their legal duty to set a rate. However, the rate set by Liverpool did not cover its spending commitments and following finance officers' advice that council staff could not be paid (the local authority was the city's largest employer), the council issued redundancy notices to its staff. The failure of Labour local authorities to win the rate-capping revolt of 1985 saw the demise of Militant on Merseyside (a leadership-led purge later removed it altogether from the Labour

Party) and, as previously argued, the end of the new urban left era in local government.

Many Labour authorities had proved themselves quite adept at annoying the Tory government through their extravagant spending and metropolitan liberal attitudes to education, policing and the arts. A special place in history must surely be reserved, however, for the GLC in its Livingstone incarnation. Livingstone, elected GLC leader in 1981 in a *coup d'état* in the GLC Labour group, was the only GLC leader in its 21-year history not to receive a knighthood – a telling fact in itself (although he probably wouldn't have accepted it anyway).

The GLC was designed during Harold Macmillan's tenure as Prime Minister to accommodate the more Conservative-inclined outer London suburbs. The Tories' strategy was successful and the GLC was ostensibly a Tory institution throughout the bulk of its relatively short lifespan, giving London such colourful characters as Sir Horace Cutler, Livingstone's predecessor as leader. Again, the period is best known for the tabloid vilification of 'Red Ken' and his Women's Committee, anti-apartheid campaigns, Nicaraguan-coffee-selling canteens, sponsorship of gay and lesbian groups and links with the IRA and the PLO. It is true that Livingstone was responsible for a wider cultural and political agenda than that which the GLC's mandate actually allowed for, but most tabloid hacks were over-generous in terms of the emphasis that they thought the GLC placed on these issues.

However, Livingstone did steer the authority on a collision course with central government and quite often deliberately set out to provoke the ire of Thatcher and the rest of the Conservative Party assembled in Parliament across the Thames from County Hall. The two areas in which the GLC earned its radical policy spurs were transport and unemployment. Its 'Fares Fair' policy of cheap public transport was, for obvious reasons, popular with Londoners but ruled as illegal in the House of Lords. It also challenged the Tories' belief that only the free market could lower unemployment (the GLC actually displayed the number of the capital's unemployed on the front of County Hall) by setting up the interventionist Greater London Enterprise Board or 'Gleb'.

The Conservatives couldn't stomach the sight of municipal socialism in their Westminster backyard and set about abolishing the GLC. Thus in 1986, after only twenty-one years of existence, the GLC was airbrushed out of history, leaving London as the only capital city in the West not to enjoy a representative tier of government as its responsibilities were shared out between the boroughs, the City of London Corporation, five government departments and sixty quangos and committees.

The antics elsewhere of the municipal socialists had certainly not gone unnoticed by the Tory government and it was widely felt that something should be done. In addition to the GLC, the Conservatives abolished the six metropolitan county councils that served the large cities and their surroundings in the provinces of the north and Midlands (South Yorkshire Metropolitan County Council was dubbed 'the People's Republic of South Yorkshire' throughout this time). It also created the Widdicombe Committee, whose remit was to get to grips with many of the tenets of municipal socialism. It found that 16 per cent of local councillors were in the employ of other local authorities, such as Hatton, who was employed by neighbouring Knowsley Borough Council in a well-paid part-time post that enabled him to be virtually a full-time politician. Therefore it recommended in its report, *The Conduct of Local Authority Business*, that senior local government officers should be debarred from also being councillors or even engaging in political activity.

The government implemented this in its Local Government and Housing Act 1989. It also inserted into its Local Government Act 1988 provisions to prevent schoolteachers from seeking to 'intentionally promote homosexuality or publish material with the intention of promoting homosexuality' or 'promote the teaching in any maintained school of the acceptability of homosexuality as a pretended family relationship' (the notorious Section 28). The Act was largely concerned with encouraging local authorities to outsource their services but the inclusion of Section 28 came about through the Conservatives' perception that 'politically correct' teachers were seeking to teach children that homosexual relationships were equally as valid as heterosexual ones, as a result of children's books such as *Jenny Lives with Eric and Martin*. The measure was one of the more controversial 'reforms' instigated by the Tories and no prosecution ever took place under it.

The Conservatives also created urban development corporations (UDCs) in several urban areas. These quangos had a fifteen-year mission to regenerate inner-city communities by market-led approaches and owed their powers to those taken from local authorities (particularly planning), although their secondary purpose was to install aspirational symbolism (luxury apartments, yachting marinas etc.) into poorer urban areas suffering post-industrial decline for partisan reasons, especially when considered alongside the non-LEA selective city technology colleges also set up for this purpose. The UDCs were a costly exercise and many people have pointed to how the funds could have been better spent by democratically elected local authorities, as many of the grandiose schemes instigated were as frivolous as anything put forward by local councils during this period. However, they, along with city technology colleges, demonstrated the Tories' wish to see the local state cut back even further and the role of local businesses increased in the provision of local services.

Education was another area of radical change by the Conservatives during this period. The reforms of Kenneth Baker in this area with the Education Reform Act 1988 altered the post-war consensus on the role of LEAs in the provision of education. In the name of increasing choice (arguably, many LEAs had begun to approach education as a purely bureaucratic exercise), the Tories set about allowing schools to opt of LEA control (giving rise to the city technology colleges mentioned above), introduced the National Curriculum, reformed school governing bodies to make them more accountable for budgets and removed polytechnics from LEAs altogether. This was packaged as allowing schools to exercise a greater degree of self-government but critics saw it as an exercise in centralisation.

During this period we became acquainted with the 'Tory flagship' councils such as Wandsworth, who in the 1980s showed the rest of local government how to behave like model local Thatcherites. One of these councils (another London borough) was the Westminster City Council of Dame Shirley Porter. Porter is now better known for her role in the 'homes for votes' scandal that engulfed Westminster in the 1990s, when it was revealed that homes had been sold in marginal Tory wards for partisan advantage during the 1980s, to the cost of £30m (for which she has famously refused to pay most of the surcharge levied against her by the district auditor).

Critics of the new urban left were wont to point out its unstinting belief in political correctness and increased spending as a panacea for all ills. The Local Government Act 1988 largely put paid to both of these ideas. Firstly, as we have seen, the inclusion of Section 28 drew a line in the sand for the bounds of local authority 'political correctness'. Secondly, the Act was also concerned with the introduction of compulsory competitive tendering (CCT). CCT was an attempt to maximise private-sector involvement in the provision of local services on one hand, and a desire to make existing local authority service departments more efficient on the other.

The Tories were frustrated that Labour authorities did not share the zeal or even the inclination to subject their services to competitive tendering with Tory councils such as Wandsworth. Instead, Labour councils cited social considerations for keeping their services in house. The Conservative environment secretary, Nicholas Ridley, wanted to transform local government from its role as a service provider to an 'enabling' body that met merely to dole out contracts for local services to the private sector. CCT was phased into existence gradually to allow for the compulsory outsourcing of local authority cleaning, maintenance and catering services (1988), sports and leisure facilities (1989), and financial and technical services (1992). Local authority direct service organisations now had to compete alongside private firms for local authority contracts. This was arguably the zenith of the New Right project for local government.

The Major years

The last major local government reform of Margaret Thatcher's Conservative administration was as concerned with financial efficiency as any of her others. It would also prove to be a tragic mistake even by the Tories' own admission. The Thatcher government was determined to curb what it perceived to be the excesses of the local state and had year on year enacted at least one Local Government Act throughout the 1980s and transferred a number of key responsibilities (higher education, urban renewal) to quangos. Furthermore it was determined to make local authorities more accountable for their spending and to instil a 'client culture' into service provision.

CCT and rate capping could only go so far in achieving this, and so the community charge (the so-called 'poll tax') was devised, packaged as the means to achieve greater accountability for local authority spending and the final step change towards a client–service provider relationship by abolishing the rates system. Pushed through in 1988, despite considerable internal opposition within the Conservative Party, the poll tax was a flat-rate levy (regardless of ability to pay), payable by all adult residents in a local authority area. However, opposition to the tax was immense, not least from the general public (manifesting itself in mass non-payment and the poll tax riots in London in 1990) but also local government itself (several Labour councillors even went to prison for refusal to pay). By 1990, Thatcher was gone from 10 Downing Street and her successor, John Major, resolved to replace it. One of Thatcher's challengers to the Conservative leadership, Michael Heseltine, was appointed environment secretary in Major's first government and was charged with finding a replacement. After considerable debate, Heseltine proposed the council tax (based on property values as opposed to individuals), which remains in place today.

Aside from abolishing the poll tax, one of Heseltine's first actions as environment secretary was to consult on the boundaries for new unitary authorities, as the government was keen to oversee more reform and a reduction in the number of local authorities. Under the Local Government Act 1992, the government established the Local Government Commission, headed by Sir John Banham, to examine the possibilities for reform of the local government structure in England (there were separate commissions for Scotland and Wales) in order to bring about unitary local authorities across Britain. The commission held a series of inquiries, deliberating at length (from 1992 to 1995), and was charged with recommending the most acceptable proposals for unitary authorities across the country. The government's preference was for single-tier all-purpose unitary authorities throughout the country (akin to the metropolitan and London boroughs since 1986), ending the two-tier system created in 1974. It believed that these would be more efficient, focused and coherent and would end duplication of provision and confusion amongst the public. However, this was not what the commission ended up recommending, as we will see later.

Reorganisation is the main legacy of the Major years as far as local government is concerned. The government's preference for unitary authorities was clear, but so was the preference of the status quo by local government itself. In Scotland and Wales, where the lack of Tory MPs exerting pressure for the retention of county councils was minimal, the task of recommending a system of unitary authorities was far simpler than in England. Scotland's nine regional and fifty-three district councils were scrapped in favour of thirty-two new unitary councils, which came into existence in 1995. In Wales, the number of councils went down from eight counties and thirty-seven districts to just twenty-two unitary authorities. In both countries, the government's plans were met with stern opposition, from trade unions, the Labour Party and, of course, local government itself. However, the new system was pushed through easily enough. In England it was an altogether different story. The 'unloved' artificial counties of Avon, Cleveland and Humberside were brushed aside with a stroke of the legislative pen after only twenty-two years in existence. The commission had a far harder task in finding acceptable proposals for the other counties it had to consider. On paper, the exercise consisted of deciding which districts or counties could take over all local government in their area and where new authorities would have to be carved out on the map.

However, in seeking to find a balance between what already existed and the new desired unitary authorities, conflict of opinion was inevitable, as to define boundaries that are smaller than a county but larger than a district entails both tiers losing out. In particular it was difficult to create viable unitary authorities in rural areas. The result was, unlike in Scotland and Wales, a dog's breakfast in terms of the hybrid system offered in England. There was to be no comprehensive single-tier layer of unitary local authorities. In some areas the counties and districts were retained, but in most cases the new unitary authorities (such as Peterborough and York) sat like islands in the middle of two-tier counties. With the loss of Avon, Cleveland and Humberside came the return of Herefordshire, Rutland and the East Riding of Yorkshire (absent as counties since the 1960s and 1970s but restored as unitary authorities).

However, the exercise was largely seen by many as a flop in terms of not delivering upon its terms of reference to recommend a comprehensive set of unitary local authority boundaries across Britain. The workings of the commission were subject to the intervention of more than one Cabinet minister and by the end of the process the government had lost its initial enthusiasm for reform.

This was acute in the light of hostile public opinion (against well-known council areas 'disappearing off the map') and Tory rural backbenchers defending the interests of county councils, all of this taking place at a time when the government was sliding in the opinion polls and dependent on a wafer-thin parliamentary majority.

Throughout the 1980s, the relationship between central and local government had been marked by tension over the transferral of local government's powers and responsibilities to unelected quangos and Major's government proved no exception to this. In 1973 the Heath government took away the last remaining responsibilities of local authorities in the sphere of health services. With the National Health Service and Community Care Act 1990 the Major government stripped away the final vestiges of influence that local authorities might have had in this area by removing them from the boards of health authorities.

There was more 'reform' with the Further and Higher Education Act 1992, which removed local authority further education and sixth form colleges from LEA control and placed the new further education corporations (the independent corporate bodies administering each individual college) under the watchful eye of Whitehall and its Further Education Funding Council (a similar body was also established to fund the former LEA polytechnics taken out of LEA control in 1988). It was argued that this would lead to more choice for students in terms of the ability to vary and extend the courses on offer locally, and that a more 'business-like' approach in terms of running the corporations would lead to greater efficiency than was the case under LEA control. The extension of choice in education was the rationale behind the Education Act 1993, which also extended the provisions of the Education Act 1988 and allowed more schools to opt out of local authority control into grant-maintained status. Again, critics saw this as the erosion of local democratic control of schools and a further extension of the quango state begun with the creation of UDCs and training and enterprise councils (TECs). The increasing number of councils in the hands of Labour were suspicious and disdainful of these bodies, many without local authority representation, and set up 'quango com-mittees' to monitor them. Other 'reforms' of the era saw local authority representation on police authorities halved and the privatisation of the local authority careers service.

The local elections of May 1995 were something of a high-water mark for the Labour Party in terms of electoral showing, the poll being, in effect, a plebiscite on the Major government's performance. Following the honeymoon period after Tony Blair's ascendancy to the Labour leadership, it was widely anticipated that Labour would win the subsequent general election and work was already in train on formulating policies for government. In particular, the Labour Party was forging a radical constitutional agenda, including the devolution of power to Scotland, Wales and the English regions and as such was seeking consensus on devolution.

The independent Commission for Local Democracy (chaired by Simon Jenkins) played a minor part in that process, although its creation was at the behest of local government in order to stimulate a debate around the future role of local authorities following tension between the centre and local government and the Tories' 'rolling back' of the local state. Its report, *Taking Charge: The Rebirth of Local Democracy* (1995), was influential on some aspects of future local government thinking such as elected mayors, as we will see in later chapters.

New Labour and the Blair era

When Tony Blair and New Labour were first elected in May 1997 in what can be regarded as the beginning of a new chapter in Britain's political history, it had the momentum of eighteen years in opposition behind it. However, the plans for local government once in office had changed substantially over the course of those years, reflecting the policies of three party leaders who held office before Blair. While the Labour Party might have reached something of a nadir in the 1983 general election and had its confidence dented in the following two, its position in local government remained at a constant strength – from the new urban left in the 1980s to the high-water mark poll of 1995 at the height of John Major's unpopularity. In fact, the only loss to Labour prestige during this period was the abolition in 1986 of councils it held – the GLC and the metropolitan counties (an action it was hardly blameworthy of, save for providing the impetus for abolition to central government). A particular shift came under Blair's leadership, when the modernising tendencies in the Labour Party revised longstanding policies overnight, including plans for both reversing Tory policy on local government and introducing regional government in England.

While New Labour had been meticulous in its overhaul of policy and image at national level (becoming 'on message'), locally some remnants of the former era remained as an embarrassment. In Walsall in 1995, at the high point of Blair's media-staged battle over the Clause 4 of the Labour constitution, 'Citizen Dave' Church became council leader after being re-elected to the council after a brief absence and committed the council to a massive programme of radical decentralisation, moving all council services away from the town hall and into neighbourhoods at some cost. The response from New Labour was swift and decisive. Church was suspended then expelled and councillors who remained loyal to him also fell to the same fate. The council has since been graded the worst in England by the Audit Commission and is no longer controlled by Labour. Similarly, the rumbling expenses scandals in South Yorkshire, where councillors on the ruling Labour groups in Doncaster and Rotherham were jailed for abusing their allowances, also proved acutely embarrassing to the party nationally. In Rotherham, the council leader was jailed after using money meant for an anti-poverty campaign to fund a lavish lifestyle, including visits to prostitutes. The Doncaster scandal was to some extent wider in its impact, with a large number of councillors falsifying expenses claims and a smaller cabal of members involved in siphoning funds and granting planning permission in exchange for bribes. In the aftermath of the revelations, which took several years to come to court, a number of councillors and members of the network received jail sentences for their involvement in the worst incidence of local government corruption since the Poulson era. Doncaster council, though headed by an elected mayor from the Labour Party, has since slid from Labour control, which could be viewed as unusual given its status as a Labour heartland, were it not for the scandal.

Coinciding with the creation of the new Local Government Association (LGA) (from the merger of the county, district and metropolitan associations) on 1 May 1997, a new department of state was created to carry deputy Prime Minister John Prescott's portfolio in charge of the environment, transport, regional and local government – the Department for Environment, Transport and the Regions (his 'super-ministry'), thus replacing the Department of the Environment (where local government had resided since Heath). This early air of co-operation between a Labour government and Labour-dominated local councils was reflected in the Central–Local Partnership, a forum for central and local government designed to provide a more balanced relationship (as opposed to the antagonisms felt between previous Tory administrations and an increasingly Labour-dominated local government). The partnership has continued to meet every six months throughout the three administrations of the Blair government, though the co-operation dwindled following several flashpoints between the government and local councils (most notably over capping and education funding) and the Conservative advance in the LGA over the course of several sets of local elections.

In finding an alternative model to CCT, which began under Margaret Thatcher and gathered pace under Major (with threatened ministerial intervention in those councils not at one with the agenda), Labour opted to revise its opposition to the concept by accepting that the market-testing culture was not only here to stay in local government but could also deliver efficiency and better services for communities. That replacement, 'Best Value', introduced in 1999 under the terms of the first Local Government White Paper (1998), accepted some of the terrain introduced under CCT but with a less rigid approach to contracting out and the overriding duty to secure 'best value' for local residents rather than outsource at all costs in the name of free-market dogma. The mantra of modernisation in this area is that councils weren't 'the only team on the pitch' and that outsourcing could be a means of partnership in a local mixed economy rather than the divisive process it had become under the Tories. However, while Best Value is more accepted within local government than its predecessor, the debate has shifted to monitoring council performance through target setting rather than hoping private firms could make gains that would benefit service users and council tax payers. A strident criticism of the Best Value regime early on was the reliance on management consultants at great public cost in ushering in the regime locally.

The Labour Party had also moved on from its opposition to the right to buy council homes and instead relied on the rallying charge of allowing local authorities to reinvest the receipts of homes sold to tenants. This remained a key demand of the left for some time. One of Labour's first acts in government was to legislate to allow local authorities to borrow against their capital receipts (subject to usual central controls) but blanket permission to spend in order to finance the building of replacement housing stock was not forthcoming. Similarly, the key demand for a power of general competence for local authorities (the continental norm whereby local councils are permitted to do anything not prohibited by statute) was quietly dropped and this instead became the new power to promote the environmental, social and economic wellbeing of a locality, promised in Labour's 1997 general election manifesto (and legislated for in 2000). The Blair government also signed the

European Charter of Local Self-Government (something the Conservatives had always refused to do) within days of entering office, though to this date it has not enacted any of the provisions contained in the charter concerned with granting more local autonomy, and a number of recent policies directly flout it.

Much was made of Thatcher's supposed formative experience of local government when her father, an alderman in her hometown of Grantham, was unceremoniously dumped by victorious Labour councillors after the local elections of 1946. Similarly, it has been said of Blair that a decision by his local Labour Party in Hackney during the early 1980s not to select him as a Labour council candidate created an abiding impression of local government within him. Upon becoming Labour leader in 1994, following the death of John Smith, Blair's intellectual energies were concentrated upon reforming what he viewed as the party's monolithic commitment to public ownership in the form of Clause 4 of its constitution. A quiet shift was also taking place in the rapid abandonment of policies around the state and the machinery of government, with previous commitments to reverse Tory policy in these areas abandoned in favour of rhetoric about modernisation and renewal rather than knee-jerk reversal. Given the mood in the party following three consecutive election defeats, Blair and his supporters were given an almost free rein to redefine policy, especially after the mandate for change delivered under the 1995 vote to modernise Clause 4 along very vague lines (though even then some dissent existed among Labour MPs and councillors).

Another way of viewing this is that Blair and New Labour began to appreciate that reversing Tory policy (i.e. returning the GLC to serve London, abolishing CCT etc.) was not a responsible approach, after a decade and a half out of power and with Tory policy already embedded and functioning (if not necessarily working), and that a more mature approach would be to modernise where necessary. As such, the reforms that began to emanate as part of Blair's ongoing review of the Labour Party acquired the badge of 'democratic renewal' (modernisation as a message tended to be directed at Labour members, not the electorate). To carry out these reforms Blair turned to those within the policy-making community and chattering classes, who had previously been dismissed by Neil Kinnock as 'whiners, whingers and wankers', in order to engage a possible progressive consensus around these policies. This had the twin benefit of appearing radical while ditching the more municipal socialist outlook so associated with the party during the 1980s. In tandem with reform going on elsewhere in the constitution (the Human Rights Act, the Freedom of Information Act, devolution to Scotland and Wales), local government was experiencing something of a fast-paced generational revolution of its own. The reforms introduced by the Conservatives between 1979 and 1997 eroded much of local government's power and prestige, but in the main they were directed at specific areas of local government's operations and not so much at the culture or overall structure itself.

One such policy associated with this era was elected mayors, an idea first floated by Michael Heseltine following his stint at the Department of the Environment but which got nowhere because of Conservative opposition to such modern thinking. In fact, to some extent, Labour entered office in 1997 equipped only with commitments to elected mayors, a new strategic body for London, Best Value (as a replacement for CCT) and a new power to promote 'economic, social and environmental wellbeing' for local councils. Elected mayors entered the policy debate as part of the independent Commission for Local Democracy's work during Labour's final days in opposition and the idea certainly chimed with New Labour's Yankophilia and the Blairite prescription of 'leadership' as a panacea for public sector failure. The idea also caught the imagination of those yearning for a more dynamic system of local democracy than the then system permitted, it having suffered the 'dented shield' under Thatcherism and having had reform foisted upon it once a generation since 1835.

The policy got its first outing in London, where the democratic deficit left by the abolition of the GLC enabled Labour to have a convenient pilot for this American-influenced new system. In 1998, the government used the local elections in the capital to stage a referendum on its proposals for a new Greater London Authority (GLA), made up of a city-wide mayor and a 25-member assembly, as a strategic form of governance for the Greater London region. This also doubled up as effectively the first trial of English regional government. In the referendum, 72 per cent of voters in the capital assented to the government's proposals, with the Conservatives in favour of the mayor but opposed to the assembly and the Liberal Democrats vice versa. One Labour figure opposed to the concept was Ken Livingstone, who hankered for the return of the GLC, preferably at County Hall (which had since been sold off to make way for a hotel and art gallery) and neither the GLA nor subsequent mayoral experiments found much favour with Labour backbenchers. Having piloted through the GLA, with an Act second only in length to the Government of India Act 1935, the government sought to bring about elected mayors outside the capital, citing major cities such as Birmingham, Manchester and Liverpool as the next candidates. In all eventuality, London ended up with a mayor not of the Prime Minister's liking (Livingstone, elected as an independent) and both the candidate selection processes and the subsequent elections demonstrated how the new system rewrote the rules to an extent which made most activists jittery.

Labour's desire to see more cities try the mayoral model found legislative form in the Local Government Act 2000, which also introduced the Standards Board for England and local frameworks as a means by which to reassure the public that Labour was serious about promoting probity in local democracy. The mayoral referendums will be covered in later chapters but the effect of the policy was to see elected mayors not in Birmingham and Manchester but Hartlepool and Mansfield. The Act was certainly monumental in scope, a landmark up there with the 1972 and 1835 Acts. Its effect on local government culture was considerable, moving away from the antiquated committee system that had been in place since 1835 and instead relying on a more leadership-based concept of governance, with scrutiny by backbench councillors to further quality decision making. However, many councillors refused to take their scrutiny role seriously, arguing that it meant a demotion from their previous role in committee making policy rather than just scrutinising it after the event. As part of this new duty to scrutinise, councils were now expected to broaden the scope of their remit to include other local public sector providers, such as the NHS. In a belated gesture to appease those opposing the controversial plans to axe community health councils (local NHS watchdogs), ministers took advantage of the new role of local government and added health scrutiny to the workload.

Another telling sign of the distance travelled by New Labour was the Crime and Disorder Act 1998, which created a statutory role for local authorities in community safety. Only a decade before, some London boroughs had set up police committees to monitor the behaviour of the Metropolitan Police in the wake of the Scarman inquiry and the breakdown in community relations that led to the Brixton riots in 1981 and those at Broadwater Farm four years later. Now, under this Act, crime and disorder reduction partnerships were established to give councils a formal role in New Labour's law and order agenda ('tough on crime, tough on the causes of crime'). Partnership between councils and the police is now so routine as to be non-noteworthy but this was not always the case. Local councils were also enlisted as part of New Labour's 'respect agenda' later in the Blair administration (particularly under the Clean Neighbourhoods and Environment Act 2005) and are constantly cited as a key agency alongside the police in tackling anti-social behaviour.

In terms of education, while Labour under Kinnock and John Smith had run policy on entirely oppositional lines, the New Labour approach could be described as acceptance and consolidation. The education action zones (which targeted intervention on poorly performing LEAs and tried to involve business in the running of schools) were to some extent beyond Tory policy. The School Standards and Framework Act 1998 affirmed New Labour's belief in inspection and intervention as a means of driving up school performance, which was hardly surprising given Blair's 'education, education, education' mantra of the time. Ministers were also given powers to take over failing schools and even LEAs. No return was made to the days of comprehensive schooling for all, with only a lukewarm and virtually unworkable approach of allowing parents local referendums on selection, and while no new city technology colleges were built, none were abolished. All of this early policy eventually found its way into the much-derided programme of city academies, where new schools were built on the proviso of external investment in their construction, which then translates into influence over the curriculum (in some cases by investors with creationist beliefs), and the plans for independent 'trust' schools and ring-fenced LEA budgets (which represented something of a major flashpoint in the breakdown of central–local relations in 2003). As for Conservative policy actually rescinded, this extended largely to the abolition of the Training and Enterprise Councils (quangos responsible for post-16 training and economic development) and their replacement, in part, by the Learning and Skills Councils, with increased local authority representation. At best, this represented an acceptance of the terrain left by the Tories and an updating of it, rather than an entirely new approach.

Labour also overhauled the regime for awarding the annual revenue support grant to each local authority, moving from the old system of the standard spending assessment to the formula spending share system, which was said to favour poorer areas (see Chapter 6). Of Labour's second-term achievements in reforming local government, the Local Government Act 2003 created new business improvement districts, freed up local authorities to borrow money, provided it could be proven to be 'prudential' in terms of repayments (i.e. not a blanket permission to borrow) under a new prudential code and gave the new comprehensive performance assessment (CPA) a legislative footing. Though the borrowing freedom was there, local government failed to react with much enthusiasm, probably because of the restraint learnt under battles with the Conservatives. The Act, by way of a Labour backbench amendment, also legislated for the rescinding of the much-hated Section 28, under which not a single case had been brought but its pernicious effect in local government (particularly around homophobic bullying) entirely felt.

As part of the agenda to both secure 'continuous improvement' in the local public services (as local government was now referred to) and provide for more accountability as a means to promote better political leadership, the Labour government invested considerable capital in the CPA regime, overseen by the Audit Commission. The idea behind CPA was that its introduction would lead to increased awareness of the quality of local services by benchmarking them against those offered by other councils, thus enabling voters to note their council's performance at election time. In practice the grading exercise proved hugely divisive and those affected by poor results following inspection queried their grades, with (unsuccessful) legal challenges on a number of occasions. After the prescriptive exercise of the first round involving counties and unitary authorities, the process was softened for the entry of districts into the regime and subsequently phased out in favour of a more streamlined inspection system rather than the bureaucratic clutter of targets. It can be said that it dawned on central government that councils were able to score decent results under CPA but still remain removed from local communities and fail to deliver responsive and visible leadership.

Much of Blair's second term was taken up with minor modifications. There was nowhere near as much activity on reform as during the first term (possibly so as to let the 2000 Act bed down), with little movement on elected mayors and suchlike after the first set of elections in May 2002 took place (after this only three mayoral referendums were held before the May 2005 general election, none successful). Another possible explanation for this could be the sheer energy invested in attempting to bring about regional government on the part of the Deputy Prime Minister, John Prescott, who assumed responsibility for local and regional government with his Office of the Deputy Prime Minister in 2002 (following the June 2001 general election local government was passed between two departments of state in a year due to Cabinet reshuffles), after stagnation on this policy area during the first term.

Plans for elected regional government in England had existed since the time of Redcliffe-Maud, gaining support within Labour during the 1970s (and even among Tory wets back then) and being the subject of a Green Paper in 1976 alongside the aborted plans for Scottish and Welsh devolution. By the time of the 1992 general election, with Labour increasingly committed to measures designed to ameliorate the democratic deficit between its heartlands in Scotland, Wales and Northern England and Tory Westminster, the plans had fully fledged maturity and envisaged nothing short of a major decentralisation from Westminster. In an entirely unconnected action, the Conservative government of John Major established government offices in each region, a regionalised bureaucracy for a handful of Whitehall ministries but nothing vaguely approaching actual devolution, though it did coincide with the proliferation of regional quangos and therefore de facto unelected regional government. In common with other areas of Labour's constitutional programme, Tony Blair as the new Labour leader approached these plans with a degree of scepticism and Jack Straw, then shadow home affairs spokesman, substantially watered them down, arguing for a piecemeal approach to regional devolution through a triple-lock process of establishing regional development agencies, consent by referendum (previously not argued for) in each region and then the reorganisation of local government along unitary lines before devolution could take place. Coupled with the revised boundaries for the new regional bodies (accepting the Conservatives' new government office boundaries and not those preferred by Labour activists), the new policy was nothing short of diminution.

In government, Blair acted very cautiously in this area, despite the ardent support of the cabinet minister responsible for overseeing it. Progress was made in London, arguably because of the issue of the abolition of the GLC, but other English regions had to be content with the creation of the eight regional development agencies (mirroring those in Scotland and Wales created under the Tories) under the Regional Development Agencies Act 1998, which also ushered in appointed regional chambers (now known as regional assemblies) to oversee them. In its second term, following the intensive work on the agenda for elected mayors, the government issued a White Paper (*Your Region, Your Choice*) in 2002, which set out its intended approach of gauging support for regional government by region and proceeding where necessary. Having identified the North-East, North-West and Yorkshire & the Humber regions as the most suitable for the first wave of referendums, the government tasked the Boundary Committee for England under its 2003 Regional Assemblies (Preparations) Act with providing blueprints for the transition to unitary local government in each region. The first referendum was scheduled for the North-East, arguably the region with the most cohesive political identity and support for the concept, in November 2004 and the Electoral Commission ran an awareness campaign and funded both 'yes' and 'no' advocates. The government's proposals were soundly defeated (78 per cent voting against on a 48 per cent turnout in the all-postal poll) for a variety of reasons, including the presence of two 'no' campaigns, an inexperienced 'yes' campaign, lukewarm support from the region's Labour MPs and the government's failure to spell out effectively what the regional assembly would actually be allowed to do once elected. Subsequent pronouncements from the government stated that elected regional government for England was no longer being pursued, as reflected in Labour's 2005 general election manifesto.

In spite of the unexpected rejection of elected regional government by the voters of the North-East in 2004, regional government remains in place, with the regional development agencies continuing to be tasked with key goals on the part of various Whitehall departments. Under the reforms enacted by the Planning and Compulsory Purchase Act 2004, it was assumed that most English regions would (as with Greater London) have elected components to lend democratic legitimacy in the transition from county-based plans to the new regional strategies. However, the new regional spatial strategies (which replaced county plans, overseen by county councils) were instead drawn up by the (unelected) regional assemblies in their capacity as regional planning bodies and included not only planning but also transport and waste strategies.

One of the areas of local government culture that Labour entered office most critical of was the tendency towards 'silo mentalities' of 'departmentalism', which was evidenced in the government's advocacy of both 'joined-up' working and attacks on the 'forces of conservatism' in the public sector. This went beyond the need for a 'third way' or mere modernisation, as tangible examples existed of public service failure because of bureaucratic inertia, some as far-reaching as the case of Victoria Climbié. Climbié, a nine-year-old African immigrant on the books of the London Borough of Haringey's social services, was reported to have suffered horrific abuse at the hands of her guardians before her death in 2000, but an inability to share information between various public sector agencies led to the failure to detect the danger she was in. The Laming inquiry appointed following her death recommended greater inter-agency co-operation in the field of child protection. This, coupled with a wider agenda to promote better services for younger people often failed by the lack of co-ordination between local authority depart-ments, led to the Children Act 2004, which demands the creation of children's trusts in each local authority (county or unitary) area to serve as a unified basis for provision of education and social services as well as co-operation with local health services. In 2006 reforms to the NHS also saw primary care trusts reconfigured to largely match these boundaries as part of both the drive for rationalisation in the public sector and the desire for increased co-terminosity and strategic governance – also seen in the merged strategic health authorities, ambulance trusts, and fire control and police authorities during the Labour government's third term.

Despite the pressing need for reform, Labour ducked the issue of council tax throughout its second term, preferring instead to hold a 'balance of funding' review chaired by the relevant minister, followed by an independent inquiry chaired by a fixer (which was subsequently broadened to include council structures and therefore deferred beyond the election). In contrast to the policies pushed from 10 Downing Street, such as 'liveability', anti-social behaviour and neighbourhood governance, the Treasury conspicuously kept its faith in regional economic planning and regional structures per se. In terms of its acceptance of Conservative policy in a number of areas (with some caveats), the vision of the 'enabling authority' ironically came closest to fruition under Labour (who had opposed it rigorously in opposition). Best Value gave way to the 'earned autonomy' of 'new localism', which in turn gave way to 'double devolution'. If anything, the Labour government's legacy will be the agenda pursued under the rubric of 'sustainable communities', which, despite its empty-sounding rhetoric, did have an entire government department at its disposal and considerable political weight behind it in the form of the deputy Prime Minister. Though whether this is just the same old regeneration initiatives with different logos on the press releases remains to be seen.

Note: London

As the national legislature and seat of government are based there, London's local government has always received an unwarranted degree of attention from national politicians. As such, the role and form of local government in London have largely differed from the rest of the country. Although the accepted capital of England, London is only the de facto capital of the United Kingdom under its unwritten constitution (London is technically a region with two cities located in it, one of which, the City of Westminster, houses the legislature and seat of government).

London was certainly exposed to a greater degree of rapid urban growth (and therefore societal pressures) during the nineteenth century and this explains this pattern of political behaviour. Until the nineteenth century, 'London' was largely taken to mean the City of London (the area around the historic 'square mile' governed by the Corporation of London) and perhaps the assortment of boroughs surrounding it such as Southwark and Westminster (a city). Seemingly, as London 'expanded' into Essex, Kent, Middlesex and Surrey, each year would see another ad hoc board tacked on to the plethora that already existed and were failing to cope with the increased demand for local services. The City of London was not covered by the reforms of 1835, the Corporation of London having mounted a successful lobbying exercise against the extension of reform to within the City's boundaries. To tackle the wider problems of London governance would be to question the unelected nature of the Corporation of London and it remained untouched for another twenty years.

The 'great stink' of 1858 spurred MPs into action as the lack of decent sanitation in London was affecting the Houses of Parliament. Even then, the ensuing legislation was a compromise – the Royal Commission appointed on this occasion was of the firm belief that the unique circumstances of London merited a different approach and that a single all-purpose elected council would not be appropriate. The Metropolis Management Act 1855 had created ninety-nine parish areas, the bulk of these being grouped into districts supervised by a district board, which were responsible for the basic services such as drainage, paving and street cleaning. Above these was the Metropolitan Board of Works (MBW); its forty-five members were nominated from each of the district boards, and it was responsible for the supervision of major sanitation in the capital. Over time it accumulated more powers so that it could exercise some responsibility for housing, road improvements and the fire service. As would be expected, though, this was far from ideal. The incoherent pattern of government did not give rise to efficient services and furthermore, because of its unelected status, the MBW was lacking in legitimacy. The government's predilection for appointing ad hoc bodies in the capital, such as the London School Board and the Metropolitan Asylums Board, continued unabated. The mere fact that local government in other parts of England was being reformed and reorganised had not gone unnoticed and allegations of corruption in the MBW gave rise to a small movement for change in the capital. A coalition of groups such as the London Municipal Reform League and the Fabian socialists were part of this movement, which led to the creation of the LCC in 1889 as a result of the Local Government Act 1888, creating county councils alongside it in other parts of England.

However, the trend of appointing more administrative bodies outside the remit of the elected tier of government continued – the Metropolitan Police, burial boards and the grandly named Thames Conservancy Board. Nevertheless, the LCC quickly developed into an eminent institution in the capital. The first administration was a 'Progressive' coalition of Liberals and Fabian socialists, the latter envisaging the LCC as a body to co-ordinate municipal socialist enterprise in the capital (such as the municipalisation of gas, water, transport and docks) and wider social programmes in housing and unemployment.

This duly alarmed the Conservative government of the time, and it produced the 1899 Local Government Act, which sought to introduce a lower elected tier of twenty-eight boroughs to replace the plethora of boards and vestries that operated within the LCC's boundaries. (In time-honoured tradition, the Corporation of London remained firmly untouched.) The rationale of this move was to provide a counterweight to the LCC from below.

Despite the LCC's reputation as an efficient and dedicated authority, by the late 1950s it was widely acknowledged that London had outgrown its nineteenth-century local government institutions. A Royal Commission headed by Sir Edwin Herbert was appointed to look at ways of providing a tier of local government that covered the greater London region rather than just the inner London area that fell under the LCC's jurisdiction. The commission unanimously recommended the creation of a Greater London Council (GLC) with as many powers as possible passing to the boroughs beneath it, these being reduced to fifty-two in number. The recommendations were acted upon in the London Government Act 1963, although the government did amend the size of the proposed authority (either following lobbying by outlying districts or refusing to include others) and created only thirty-two London boroughs, with education being passed to the outlying boroughs, with education in those that were originally under the boundaries of the LCC to be supervised by a new Inner London Education Authority. The new system was in fact copied to some extent by the Local Government Act 1972 (which provided a comprehensive two-tier system along similar lines for England and Wales).

The election of Margaret Thatcher's Conservative government in 1979 was shortly followed by Labour's retaking the GLC from the Tories in 1981. The two events were significant as they signalled a collision course between the two tiers of government on ideological lines. Tensions over transport policy and the Tory-baiting antics of the GLC's leader, Ken Livingstone, saw the demand for abolition intensify (the Tory boroughs had originally argued for it in the early 1980s) and with the Local Government Act 1985, Londoners found themselves in the same situation as they would have been a century earlier, with the GLC's functions passing to either the boroughs or a plethora of government-appointed quangos.

Until the creation of the GLA (a directly elected mayor and 25-member assembly) and the subsequent election of Livingstone as mayor in 2000, London had fourteen years in the wilderness without any kind of elected representative tier of government. In addition, under the new system, the extended 'GLA family' means that bodies such as the Metropolitan Police Authority (whose functions were previously carried out single-handedly by the Home Secretary) and the new London Fire and Emergency Planning Authority have the benefit of being chaired by elected representatives of the people of London. However, governance arrangements in London remain incoherent, even post-GLA. The issues facing outer London, where, for example, Harrow has more in common with Watford in Hertfordshire, in terms of transport and education, than Lambeth in inner London, mean that London's political institutions (based on 1965 boundaries designed to electorally favour one political party) are somewhat in need of targeted reform. In 2004, the London Assembly and the thirty-three local authorities in the capital agreed to examine London governance under a special commission, which reported in 2006 and recommended wholesale reform through the strengthening of existing bodies rather than any mergers of councils. Though opposing Livingstone's election as mayor in 2000 but readmitting him in time to stand for re-election in 2004, the Labour Party then accepted the need for change to the reforms it formulated in opposition during the mid-1990s, and in its 2005 general election manifesto it proposed to give the mayor more powers over matters such as housing, training and waste.

Note: Scotland

Like many other facets of its political system, the evolution of local government in Scotland has always been closely pegged to that of England. Local administrative units, known as burghs, came into existence during the Middle Ages for the primary purpose of sustaining trade in local communities and also protecting royal revenues and influence. They eventually assumed more powers to regulate other areas of local life. Like the English parish vestries, the Scottish Church established 'kirk sessions' to provide poor relief and basic education on a parochial basis. These activities were financed by both church collections and the rates system, the rate being set on a county basis by 'commissioners of supply'. Being similar to the English quarter sessions, they eventually accumulated powers to manage highways and organise local police forces.

By the early nineteenth century, however (a century after the Act of Union with England), these unelected units had succumbed to corruption and a lack of competence to deal with the social issues of the day entailed with urban growth. Many burghs were reformed under the burghs reform Acts of 1833, although some of the smaller burghs remained untouched until 1900. The middle part of the nineteenth century saw some further reform, with the introduction of local elected poor relief boards in 1845, local boards for the care of the mentally ill in 1857 and elected school boards in 1872. Elected county councils were (as in England) introduced in 1889, and in 1900 the Town Councils (Scotland) Act ensured that all burghs were elected bodies.

In 1918, the school boards were replaced with conventional LEAs based on counties and large burghs and in 1929 the local government system was rationalised into county councils, 'counties of cities' (akin to English county boroughs), large burghs, small burghs and district councils. In 1966, a Royal Commission headed by Lord Wheatley (running alongside the Redcliffe-Maud Commission) was appointed by the Labour government of Harold Wilson to find ways of reforming the system further. The commission recommended the reform of Scottish local government along the lines of a largely two-tier system of nine regional councils and fifty-three district councils, with three unitary island councils and a tier of representative (if not entirely functional) community councils at the parish level (though not uniform in their existence). The Conservative government at Westminster accepted the commission's proposals and from 1975 this was the system of local government that operated in Scotland.

As in Wales, the round of local government reorganisation initiated under John Major's Conservative government left Scotland with a wholly unitary system of local government of thirty-two councils from 1996 onwards, axing the regional councils in favour of district councils with altered boundaries. Scottish local government has, since 1999, functioned under the control of the devolved Scottish Parliament. Possibly the biggest reform enacted by the Scottish Executive post-devolution, having resisted English modernisation measures such as elected mayors, is the introduction of the single transferable vote system of proportional representation for Scottish councils from 2007. The system, a key demand of the Liberal Democrats during coalition negotiations with Labour after the 1999 and 2003 Scottish parliamentary elections, was recommended by an independent commission.

Note: Wales

In spite of its separate history as a nation, because of Wales's longstanding historic constitutional symmetry with England, Welsh local government owes its genesis to the same circumstances as

England's and its reform has generally been carried out alongside that of England (Redcliffe-Maud for instance). There are several recent differences between Wales and England, however. Welsh elected parochial units are known as 'community councils' and, following the local government reorganisation of the mid-1990s, Wales was left with a wholly unitary system of local government with twenty-two councils, ending the two tiers of counties and districts that had been in place since 1974. The Welsh Assembly has no formal legislative powers over local government in Wales but supervises it in the same way that the Secretary of State for Wales did until the assembly became live in 1999. The assembly is currently conducting a review of local council services in Wales.

Note: Northern Ireland

Due to the size of the province and the irregular constitutional nature of Northern Ireland as part of the United Kingdom, the role and function of local government differs from that in the rest of the country. Following the Macrory Review of 1970, local government was reorganised in 1973 into twenty-six district councils (elected using proportional representation) and nine area boards (a mixture of local councillors appointed by the districts and ministerial appointees). The result of the 1973 reorganisation was the transfer of local services to central government in the province, in anticipation of a restored and more cross-community devolved government, so as to guard against any sectarian behaviour in local government (thus creating the so-called 'Macrory gap'). The traditional six counties of Northern Ireland (part of the nine counties of Ulster on the island of Ireland) are now ceremonial only. The residual functions of the district councils include leisure and environmental services, the licensing of markets and entertainments and food hygiene and trading standards. There are four area boards for health and social services and five for education and libraries. There is a single housing executive and a fire authority for the province. Since the Good Friday Agreement of 1998 and the assembly elections of 1999, other services and the general supervision of local government matters in the province are now nominally administered by the Northern Ireland Executive (or Northern Ireland Office during any suspension of devolution).

In 2005 and 2006, the Review of Public Administration, established by the Northern Ireland Executive following devolution, reported. Its recommendations, which were accepted by the Northern Ireland Office but resisted by most in local government, included reducing the number of councils in the province from twenty-six to just seven but increasing their powers in some areas (planning, environment and economic development), as well as rationalising the number of quangos responsible for local services.

2. Overview of local government in the UK

Current system of principal authorities in England as it stands at 2006 (including emergency services), with brief notes on situation in Scotland, Wales and Northern Ireland.

We have seen how local government in the United Kingdom has proceeded along distinct paths in each of its constituent nations, with England and Wales jointly arriving at a diverse and complex array of functions delegated to their local authorities. This process, which began with the Poor Law Act 1601, underwent several phases alongside the evolution of the national political system. Since 1835, with the birth of what could be considered to be local democratic institutions, the relationship between the centre and the local level has always been characterised by tension and, since 1945 at least, the gradual erosion of local autonomy and power. However, local government in England and Wales remains a key element of the national economy and its largest employer, as well as providing the highest number of elected representatives compared to other levels of government. For all the erosion of its powers and autonomy, local government remains a key provider of public services to every citizen, who will quite often use the services of different councils depending on where they live and work.

First, a word on how local government's powers are defined within Britain's unwritten constitution. While Britain's arrangements have been 'condemned by logic but approved by experience' (as Redlich and Hirst once observed), they have left a lasting impression on its former colonies, from the dominions of Canada (which retains 'ridings'), Australia and South Africa, to even the United States (New York's city council was modelled on the City of London Corporation, for instance). However, the steady erosion of local accountability and direction in public services has rendered local democracy almost impotent in the eyes of many. During the late 1980s and early 1990s, following the onslaught of Thatcherism against it, many in local government championed the idea of a 'power of general competence' as a means to promote it and guard against future erosion. The power of general competence is the norm in most European and some Commonwealth political systems, and under it local councils are free to act as they see fit, except where expressly prohibited from doing so – the exact opposite of the British system, whereby councils' power and duties are laid down by statute and operating outside of this is seen as *ultra vires* (exceeding their stated powers). The cause was taken up as part of wider efforts to modernise Britain's constitution and reinvigorate local democracy but effectively came to nothing, save for the already discussed power to 'promote economic, social and environmental wellbeing' and the lip service paid to the European Charter of Local Self-Government. Unless efforts are made towards drafting a written constitution for the UK, it is unlikely to return.

Furthermore, this characteristic centralism is underpinned by the sovereignty of Parliament, which means that at any juncture local government's existence could theoretically be swept away on the basis of a one-vote majority in the House of Commons. As the Widdicombe inquiry reported, amid one of the worst periods of centre–local relations, local government simply has no independent right to exist.

Legal framework

Having ascertained the constitutional position of local government as both a political institution and the provider of local public services, it is worth noting the raft of Acts which underpin its existence. While we have traced the origins of British local democracy back to 'time immemorial' (i.e. before 1189 by law), the first local government Act, of sorts, was the Poor Law Act 1601, which was only repealed in 1948 following the passage of the National Assistance Act. In terms of constituting local government in England and Wales, the following Acts form the bedrock of the current system (see also Appendix II):

- London: the London Government Act 1963, as amended by the Local Government Act 1985, the Education Reform Act 1988 and the Greater London Authority Act 1999
- the metropolitan areas outside London: the Local Government Act 1972, as amended by the Local Government Act 1985
- the shire areas: the Local Government Act 1972, as amended by orders made under the Local Government Act 1992
- Wales: the Local Government Act (Wales) 1994
- Wales and England outside London: the Police and Magistrates' Courts Act 1994
- All England and Wales: the Planning and Compulsory Purchase Act 2004

(Rita Hale and Anna Capaldi (eds), *Councillors' Guide to Local Government Finance*, 2005 edition, CIPFA)

There are a total of 410 local authorities in England and Wales, while there are 32 in Scotland and 26 in Northern Ireland. In Scotland, Wales and urban England single-tier unitary authorities provide all local services, whereas the remainder of England is served by a two-tier system split between district and county councils. There are 34 county councils in England and these cover a further 238 smaller district councils. In addition there are 22 unitary authorities in Wales and 116 in England, mainly serving urban areas. These unitary authorities can be broken down as in Table 2.1.

Table 2.1: Distribution of English unitary authorities

English shires	47 unitary authorities
Greater Manchester	10 metropolitan authorities
Merseyside	5 metropolitan authorities
South Yorkshire	4 metropolitan authorities
Tyne and Wear	5 metropolitan authorities
West Midlands	7 metropolitan authorities
West Yorkshire	5 metropolitan authorities
Greater London	32 London boroughs and the City of London

The metropolitan authorities assumed their current powers and status in 1986 following the abolition of the metropolitan counties alongside which they previously existed. Similarly the London boroughs and the City of London Corporation assumed their current powers and status following the abolition of the Greater London Council that year. The forty-seven unitary authorities in the English shires were created in tranches during the mid- to late 1990s following the process undertaken by the Local Government Act 1992 and the Banham Review.

Under the two-tier system, the lower tier is recognised as districts (or non-metropolitan districts), although some of these may have status as boroughs through old Royal Charters conferred upon them. This also applies to cities, although a number of boroughs have also

71

been converted or upgraded to city status more recently. All local authorities have chairmen or mayors as ceremonial/civic figureheads; in some larger and older cities they may be styled Lord Mayor. Where an authority is called a district council it will have a chairman and where the authority is a borough or city council it will have a mayor (or a Lord Mayor).

Local government boundaries owe their current basis to local government legislation, though voluntary mergers are permissible under the law, and the Boundary Committee for England is now responsible for the overall examination of local government boundaries and structures. Local government legislation accords a number of responsibilities to each type of local authority (see sections below and relevant chapters).

Cities

City status accords no extra powers in law and contrary to perception is not related to any single factor such as population size or religious significance, only the existence of a royal edict. Today city status is granted by the Crown acting on the advice of the Prime Minister, usually in connection with a specific event, though historically the decision to confer city status centred upon the monarch. Though towns referring to themselves as boroughs do so through the issuing of a Royal Charter, city status is in fact conferred by letters patent – those cities predating the English monarchy as historically constituted (before 1189) are automatically regarded as cities since time immemorial.

While city status prior to the sixteenth century was reserved solely for settlements of religious significance, since the wave of new cities in emerging industrial centres and provincial capitals during the nineteenth century (Birmingham, Leeds, Liverpool, Manchester,

Newcastle, Nottingham and Sheffield), this has not been the case. The creation of Anglican dioceses was suspended during the sixteenth century and no new cities were created for some time after this point, with the first new diocese and city being created in Ripon in 1832. After this the only religious settlements to be given city status were St David's in Wales and Armagh in Northern Ireland, both in 1994, after their status had lapsed. In 1969 Swansea became a city to mark the Prince of Wales' investiture there, while in 1977 Derby was awarded city status to mark the Queen's Silver Jubilee. The first open competition for towns to seek city status was held in 1992 to mark the Queen's fortieth anniversary as monarch and saw Sunderland become a city. For the millennium celebrations in 2000, Brighton & Hove, Wolverhampton and Inverness were granted city status, while to mark the Queen's Golden Jubilee in 2002, Preston (England), Newport (Wales) and Stirling (Scotland) were elevated to it. In Northern Ireland it was decided to award the honour to two cities, one predominantly nationalist (Newry) and one predominantly unionist (Lisburn), because of political sensitivities in the province. Most English cities have 'city councils', though their powers depend entirely on their status as district, unitary, metropolitan or London borough council.

There are also around 10,000 non-principal local authorities, known as parish and town councils in England and community councils in Wales. These fulfil a more localised role where they exist, such as the maintenance of allotments and street lighting (see section below and Chapter 11). A small number of these have the ceremonial title of city, hailing from the era under which they were boroughs in their own right prior to absorption into larger units under reorganisation. They are Chichester, Ely, Hereford, Lichfield, Ripon, Truro and Wells. See Table 2.2 for a list of English cities.

Table 2.2: English cities, including dates of incorporation (the absence of a date denotes a city since time immemorial) and, in cases where the city is a non-principal local authority, the new local authority name where it differs from that of the city (e.g. 'part of Harrogate')

Bath (1590)

Birmingham (1889)

Bradford (1897)

Brighton & Hove (2000)

Bristol (1542)

Cambridge (1951)

Canterbury

Carlisle

Chester (1541)

Chichester

Coventry (1345)

Derby (1977)

Durham

Ely (part of East Cambridgeshire)

Exeter

Gloucester (1541)

Hereford (part of Herefordshire) (1189)

Kingston upon Hull (1897)

Lancaster (1937)

Leeds (1893)

Leicester (1919)

Lichfield (1553)

Lincoln (1880)

Liverpool (1880)

City of London

Manchester (1853)

Newcastle upon Tyne (1882)

Norwich (1195)

Nottingham (1897)

Oxford (1542)

Peterborough (1541)

Plymouth (1928)

Portsmouth (1926)

Preston (2002)

Ripon (part of Harrogate) (1836)

St Albans (1877)

Salford (1926)

Salisbury

Sheffield (1893)

Southampton (1964)

Stoke-on-Trent (1925)

Sunderland (1992)

Truro (part of Carrick) (1877)

Wakefield (1888)

Wells (part of Mendip) (1205)

Westminster (1540)

Winchester

Wolverhampton (2000)

Worcester (1189)

York

Counties, districts and unitaries: powers and responsibilities

As we have seen, one of the bedrock Acts for English government is the Local Government Act 1972, which introduced the two-tier system across England and Wales of metropolitan and non-metropolitan counties and metropolitan and non-metropolitan districts. For the purposes of local government in England today, **counties** is generally taken to mean the forty-six administrative counties created in 1972 under the Local Government Act of that year. Of course, the English shire counties themselves are deeply historical, the word 'shire' being of Anglo-Saxon origin and 'county' (as in ruled by a count) of Norman; and while some historic counties no longer exist in an administrative sense they remain as ceremonial counties, each with its own lord lieutenant (as the monarch's designated local representative).

Before the 1972 Act, the first administrative counties were created in 1889 and amended only in 1965 (in the case of Greater London) before the introduction of the metropolitan and non-metropolitan counties in 1974 (as amended in 1985 with the abolition of the metropolitan counties and the Greater London Council; see below). Each of the thirty-four remaining non-metropolitan counties (also known as shire counties) has its own elected county council, elected every four years, headed by a leader and cabinet under the Local Government Act 2000, with a chairman as its civic figurehead. The primary functions associated with counties are that of education (as local education authorities) and social services, though counties also play key roles in highways, waste disposal, public transport, economic development and consumer protection. Counties were divested of their strategic planning function under the Planning and Compulsory Purchase Act 2004, which placed this function under each regional assembly when sitting as the planning body to agree the regional spatial strategy. Counties continue to raise their own local finance through the 'precept' levied on billing authorities beneath them at district level.

Under the reforms enacted in the mid-1990s as part of the last round of local government reorganisation originally designed to introduce an entirely unitary pattern of local government across Britain, **unitary authorities** were created between 1995 and 1998 to undertake the roles formerly designated for counties alongside those already undertaken by the districts. Unitary authorities had already existed in the form of London boroughs and metropolitan districts following the abolition of the GLC and the six metropolitan county councils under the Local Government Act 1985. The Isles of Scilly Council as neither a county or district but created under the 1972 Act was technically a unitary but a *sui generis* one at that. The new unitary authorities created between 1995 and 1998 resemble their precursors but are not usually banded with them legally because of the different legislation required to establish them (though they are henceforth known collectively in this book as 'single-tier authorities'). As such, single-tier authorities currently discharge all services undertaken by councils in the remaining two-tier shire areas and are billing authorities in that they set and collect their own council tax.

The non-metropolitan **districts** (which may also be known as boroughs; see sections above) are the sub-county tier which was also introduced in the 1972 Act and have largely remained unaltered, save for those which became unitaries between 1996 and 1998. English districts in shire areas are largely responsible for environmental, waste, housing and planning services.

For a breakdown of which authorities provide which services, see Table 2.3.

Emergency services

Police and fire were traditional areas of local authority activity at the county level following the reforms undertaken in the 1830s and the mandatory provision of policing in 1856, overseen at that time by magistrates until the creation of the administrative counties in 1889. Following reorganisations in 1946 and 1964, police authorities in England and Wales were made independent of the counties under the Police and Magistrates Courts Act 1994 and Police Act 1996, which created independent police authorities consisting of nominated councillors, independent appointees and magistrates. Most of the force and authority areas enjoyed some co-terminosity with county boundaries, though some joint arrangements exist where this is not possible (for instance Leicestershire county and Rutland unitary under Leicestershire Police). Joint arrangements also exist in Scotland, save for two unitary council areas where the police authority and unitary authorities share the same boundary. Policing in Greater London for the Metropolitan Police Service area (excluding the City of London) is supervised by the Metropolitan Police Authority, a functional body of the Greater London Authority. Under reforms tabled in 2006, the current county-based police authorities for England and Wales would be merged into new largely regionalised 'strategic' areas, though at the time of writing the plans had been shelved. The British Transport Police operate under separate national arrangements, including in the Metropolitan Police area (on London Underground, for instance).

Table 2.3: Services by tier

	Joint authorities	Metropolitan authorities	London boroughs	Unitary authorities	County councils	District councils
Development control		*	*	*		*
Education		*	*	*	*	
Electoral administration		*	*	*		*
Environmental health		*	*	*		*
Highways		*	*	*	*	
Housing		*	*	*		*
Leisure and recreation		*	*	*		*
Passenger transport	*			*	*	
Revenue collection		*	*	*		*
Social services		*	*	*	*	
Waste collection		*	*	*		*
Waste disposal	*	*	*	*	*	

Each local council may, subject to approval, consider a change to its place name (e.g. Merton) but not status as a district (to borough, for instance). Similarly, two districts may also propose to merge, subject to approval.

The fire brigades in England and Wales also owe their origins to municipal and county councils from the mid-nineteenth century but were reorganised into a National Fire Service during the Second World War. After the war the Fire Services Act 1947 restored them to local government at the county and county borough level, with reorganisation in 1974 under the Local Government Act 1972 (and in 1986) reducing their number. Though fire and rescue authorities as bodies of nominated local councillors currently exist on a county or joint basis (in the case of new unitaries), recent reforms to fire control centres have seen some degree of regional reorganisation, alongside Regional Management Boards. In Greater London, the London Fire and Emergency Planning Authority is responsible for fire services across its jurisdiction as a functional body of the Greater London Authority.

Local government was stripped of its remaining healthcare responsibilities in the form of ambulance provision in 1974.

Sub-principal authorities

The local authorities created under the Local Government Act 1972 are designated 'principal authorities', though a historic and variable tier of around 7,800 sub-principal authorities also exists. Parish and town councils owe their existence to the ancient network of ecclesiastical parishes which operated under the stewardship of the Church of England as an early unit of local government (as early as 1555 concerning highway upkeep and then under the Poor Law Act 1601). The link between the ecclesiastical parishes and the civil parishes was severed with the Local Government Act 1894. Not all of England is covered by parishes – they were abolished in Greater London in 1965 in the shake-up of local government in the capital and further changes in 1974 saw many phased out in most urban areas. Under the Local Government and Rating Act 1997, new parishes may be created where residents demand this under an agreed process of petition, referendum and central government approval, and the Labour Party manifesto of 2005 promised to increase their powers over anti-social behaviour and to lift the legislative bar on their creation in London.

In the case of urban areas, parishes may style themselves 'town councils', with their own mayor. The largest town council is Weston-super-Mare, with a population of almost 72,000. However, some parishes cover areas with populations of less than 100. The responsibilities of parishes vary according the wishes of those establishing them and their powers can be increased on application to central government. Broadly speaking, most parishes concern themselves with street scene operations and the upkeep of communal green space and some associated functions (allotments and community halls, for instance). Parishes are also entitled to be consulted on planning issues by the district and unitary councils above them. They are financed by a precept levied on billing authorities, which does lead to some animosity of accountability over spending decisions and resistance to the creation of new parishes in some instances. Parish councils are subject to four-yearly elections, though these will only be held if there are more candidates than available seats and on many occasions there is no election. Where too few candidates come forward, the council may co-opt new members unless ten or more residents request an election. As such and coupled with their lack of uniformity (parished and unparished areas) across England, this has led many to treat sub-principal authorities as not worthy of serious consideration. Recent efforts on the part of their national association (the National Association of Local Councils) and central government to re-establish their reputation has seen the Quality Parish initiative, to recognise those councils who deliver good services and adhere to full democracy.

In Scotland and Wales, parish and town councils do not exist, having been replaced by community councils, created under the Local Government Act 1972 and Local Government (Scotland) Act 1973. Unlike England, all of Wales is divided into communities, though elected community councils only exist where demanded. In Scotland, community councils only exist in a number of areas and as a representative forum rather than a service delivery body with precepting powers.

Scotland, Wales and Northern Ireland

The differences between English unitaries and their thirty-two Scottish counterparts, which have existed since 1996, are largely titular, though by dint of the supervision of local government by the devolved Scottish Executive and the centuries-old separate local government system, there are some differences in relation to powers, duties and nomenclature that are too numerous to list here in a book concerned primarily with England. For instance, the head of a Scottish council is known as the provost or convenor and is elected for four years, as opposed to English civic mayors and their annual terms of office. The Scottish Executive decided not to emulate the governance reforms carried out in England and Wales in 2000. Scotland's unitaries are elected all-out every four years, though the elections scheduled for 2007 will be the first held under the single transferable vote system.

The role and structure of the twenty-two Welsh unitary authorities, which have also existed since 1996, are identical to the English unitaries, though some style themselves as counties (Powys), county boroughs (Blaenau Gwent) or joint counties and cities (Cardiff). While they may resemble English unitaries, the Welsh councils are under the supervision of the devolved Welsh Assembly government at Cardiff rather than the Department for Communities and Local Government in London. Elections to the Welsh unitaries take place at the same time every four years.

Like Scotland, Northern Ireland has a different legal and constitutional relationship to the rest of the United Kingdom. Northern Ireland is currently divided into twenty-six district council areas, created under the Northern Ireland Constitution Act 1973 following the 1970 Macrory Review. The review assumed the continuation of the devolved administration at Stormont and, reflecting community tensions, argued that services such as education and housing were best administered either at provincial or joint board level in order to avoid the sectarianism in public service provision that led to the outbreak of the Troubles in 1969. As such, the districts are largely responsible for street scene, community and environmental services, whereas education, social services and housing are administered either by province-wide agencies or nominated joint boards, under the supervision of the Northern Ireland Civil Service and the Northern Ireland Executive (when functioning). Public sector employment is also unusually high in the province due to its lack of other employment sources. In 2005 the Review of Public Administration recommended to ministers the merging of the twenty-six districts into just seven new 'super-councils' and the streamlining of quangos in the province as means to bridge the 'democratic deficit' and reduce the province's over-governance and dependency on public employment. The review's recommendations were accepted and should be in place in time for the scheduled 2009 elections. Elections to the current districts take place every four years on an all-out basis and use the single transferable vote system. Unusually, Northern Ireland retains the practice of electing aldermen, which was discontinued on the mainland in 1972.

3 Elected members and elections

The role of the councillor, legal duties, method of election etc. Standards framework, voter registration. New arrangements under Local Government Act 2000, including elected mayors, cabinets and scrutiny.

Since it is local government we are considering, the elected element is paramount. Elected local councillors have been the bedrock of modern local government since its creation in 1835 and the regular selection of eligible local representatives with whom to entrust the oversight of local public services remains at the core of the system. Considered in its entirety, English local government is under the supervision of almost 20,000 locally elected councillors sitting on principal-tier local authorities. This section will detail how they are elected and their responsibilities within the system of local governance.

The legal position

The principal legislation for the conduct of local elections in England is:

- Representation of the People Act 1983
- Registration of Political Parties Act 1998
- Local Government Act 2000
- Political Parties, Elections and Referendums Act 2000
- Representation of the People Act 2000.

Eligibility to vote in local elections in Britain is largely the same as for all other public elections. The main criteria for inclusion on the electoral register, maintained by electoral registration officers (EROs) in district- and unitary-level authorities, is that voters should be:

- aged eighteen years or older on election day;
- citizens of the United Kingdom or the Republic of Ireland;
- not subject to any legal incapacity to vote.

Legal incapacities include membership of the House of Lords (though peers can still vote in local, devolved and European elections), EU or Commonwealth citizenship (though such citizens may vote in all but parliamentary elections), citizens of any other country, convicted prisoners, those detained on mental health grounds and those convicted of an electoral offence in the last five years. By law the ERO must strive to ensure that all eligible persons in their district are included on the annual register, which also includes overseas voters and those who have chosen to vote by post. Postal voting on demand has been available since 2000, having previously been available only to those with a documented reason (the infirm, for instance).

On the basis of the electoral register of voters, elections are held for each council on differing cycles of four-year terms, depending on the type of authority, as in Table 3.1.

Table 3.1: Elections cycle

Type of authority	Electoral cycle and warding arrangements	2003	2004	2005	2006	2007
County councils	Full council elections. Single-member electoral divisions.			Full council		
London boroughs	Full council elections. Multimember wards.				Full council	
Metropolitan districts	By thirds. All wards have three members.	1/3	1/3		1/3	1/3
88 shire districts and various unitaries	By thirds. Almost all wards have 1–3 members.	1/3	1/3		1/3	1/3
150 shire districts and various unitaries	Full council elections. Almost all wards have 1–3 members.	Full council			Full council	
Welsh unitaries	Full council elections. Around half are single member.		Full council			

Source: Local Government Association

County council divisions are always represented by a single councillor. Multi-member wards (generally with three members, sometimes two) are the norm in unitaries, London boroughs, metropolitan boroughs and in the urban parts of district councils. Wards in rural parts of district councils generally have a single member. All local elections take place on the first Thursday in May. If a councillor dies or resigns during their term of office, a by-election is held in their ward to elect a replacement.

In England and Wales, local elections are held under the first-past-the-post system. The candidate with the highest number of votes is elected, or in the case of multi-member wards, the two or three top candidates. It is only necessary to be ranked first, not to gain 50 per cent or more of the total votes cast. Indeed, in contests where three or more parties stand, the winning candidate frequently receives less than 50 per cent of the votes cast.

It is a legal requirement for those standing as candidates for local authorities in the United Kingdom to be:

- aged eighteen years or older on the day of nomination;
- a British, Commonwealth or EU citizen;
- registered to vote for that particular local authority or at least to have lived, owned land or premises, or worked in the local authority area for the previous twelve months.

Those disqualified from standing as a candidate in local government elections include:

- employees of the local authority holding the elections;
- those regarded as working in politically restricted local authority posts elsewhere;
- those subject to bankruptcy restrictions;
- those having served a prison sentence of three months or more in the past five years.

If a person meets the criteria outlined above, then in order to contest the election they must file nomination papers with the local authority's returning officer by the date given on the notice of election (usually around one month before the poll). The nomination papers must be signed by ten electors resident in the ward being contested. The returning officer then publishes a statement of persons nominated and a notice of election agents' names and offices a few days later.

The rules concerning candidates representing a political party (the most common form of candidature) were tightened following incidents of fraudulent or misleading claims on the ballot paper (the oft-cited Literal Democrat, for instance). Such candidates may use a party description of up to six words and a registered party logo on the ballot paper. This must be verified by the party's nominating officer (or their representative locally). Candidates not standing on a party ticket may choose to describe themselves as an 'Independent' or give no description at all.

Nominated candidates can (and generally do) appoint an agent for their campaign. Quite often a party official will act as agent for several candidates and most parties offer training in this area. Those who do not appoint an agent are deemed to be the agent themselves. Candidates can also appoint representatives on their behalf to observe polling stations and the count on election day. Unlike other elections, no deposit is required for local elections.

One of the strictest aspects of campaign activity for election candidates is the restrictions on campaign literature, which range from spending limits to general laws concerning libel, defamation and potentially inflammatory statements. Specifically for elections, however, any official literature issued by the candidate or their agent must bear legal wording (the 'imprint') to show the printer and promoter of the literature. In 2006 the spending limits per candidate for local government elections were £600 plus 5p per elector registered in the ward. This figure also includes spending on administration and travel during the campaign and each candidate's agent must file detailed accurate returns with the returning officer within thirty-five days following the election. Failure to do so or filing fraudulent returns can lead to criminal prosecution and the subsequent forfeiture of the election in the case of winning candidates.

Polling generally takes place between 7 a.m. and 10 p.m., although under some electoral modernisation pilot schemes these hours have been varied. The staff of the returning officer responsible for administering the poll in each polling station are required to ensure the secrecy of the ballot, and candidates and their agents are legally prevented from interfering in the process. Following the close of polls, council staff count the ballots by hand (unless under a pilot scheme, such as electronic counting) until the result can be declared by the returning officer. Once the result has been announced it is final, subject to any legal challenge in the event of a miscount, and the returning officer must then publish a public notice of the election result. The winning candidate must sign their declaration of acceptance of office within two months of the election for it to be valid.

Elections policy

The turnout for local elections in Britain as an indicator of public interest and the health of local democracy has long been cause for concern both among political parties and among those with an interest in the political process. It is significantly lower than at general elections, averaging around 30–35 per cent for the best part of a generation, as Table 3.2 shows.

Measures introduced since 1997 to combat low turnouts include the modernisation of electoral registration (the rolling register and postal voting on demand) and a number of pilot schemes aimed at exploring easier ways to vote than the traditional polling station and ballot paper. Election pilots took place in a number of English local authorities in May 2000 and May 2002. In May 2000, thirty-two local councils ran a total of thirty-eight experimental voting arrangements, including postal voting on demand, all-postal ballots, voting on more than one day (including a weekend), extended polling hours, mobile polling stations and electronic voting and counting. In May 2002, thirty local authorities piloted a total of thirty-six innovative voting procedures. These included further tests of postal voting, extended voting hours and mobile polling stations, but also included some experiments in e-voting, using telephones, the Internet and text messaging. In most cases turnout demonstrably

Table 3.2: Local government election turnouts 1979–2005

Year	London	English metropolitans	English counties	English districts (w)	English districts (p)	Welsh counties	Welsh districts	Scottish regions	Scottish districts	English unitaries
1979		74.7		72.1	73.5			76.9		
1980		36.3			38.9				45.7	
1981			43.7			48.6				
1982	43.9	38.8			41.8			42.9		
1983		42.0		45.0	45.6		46.3			
1984		39.8			40.2				44.4	
1985			41.6			45.2				
1986	45.4	39.9			41.9			45.6		
1987		44.7		48.8	50.6		51.4			
1988		40.1			41.5				45.5	
1989			39.2			44.2				
1990	48.1	46.2			48.6			45.9		
1991		40.8		48.2	46.2		53.4			
1992		32.5			37.8				41.4	
1993			37.2			38.8				
1994	46.0	38.9			42.6			45.1		
1995		33.8		41.9	39.2		48.8		44.9	39.7
1996		30.5			37.2					34.6
1997			73.2							69.7
1998	34.6	24.8			30.8					27.8

In 1998 two-tier local government ended in Scotland and Wales

Year	London	English metropolitans	English counties	English districts (w)	English districts (p)	Welsh unitaries	Scottish unitaries	English unitaries
1999		26.1		35.8	32.5	49.7	59.4	31.5
2000		26.0			32.2			28.5
2001			62.5					57.6
2002	33.6	31.8			35.4			30.2
2003		32.1		35.5	31.9		49.2	34.6
2004		41.3			41.0	43.2		37.2
2005			63.8					61.3

Figures for 1995 and 1999 in both Scotland and Wales refer to turnout at the unitary council elections. Turnout data for English districts have been separately calculated for authorities that use whole-council (w) and partial (p) elections. Reliable data for Welsh local authorities are unavailable for the earlier years. (LGC Local Elections Centre, University of Plymouth) increased where voting was made simpler and in the areas trialling all-postal ballots this was even more successful (in Chorley turnout almost doubled, from 31.3 per cent to 62.5 per cent). However, the trials were halted in the wake of the postal vote abuse cases in 2004, though the government remains committed to modernising the electoral process and a smaller number of trials were undertaken at the 2006 English local elections.

The role of political parties

Most council candidates contest elections on behalf of registered political parties. Although independents do get elected (10 per cent of all councillors, mostly in rural areas), it remains the case that a party label often assists voters and enables candidates to receive campaigning support in their bid to secure election.

Once elected to the council, councillors sit in party groups that elect officers to formulate policy and maintain party discipline in the council chamber. The last council in the UK to require councillors to sit independently of groups ended this practice in 2006 (Powys). There is no legal requirement to remain in the same party once elected and defections between parties on issues of principle and/or party discipline do happen from time to time. The three main parties have councillors' associations at national level to provide routine assistance and liaison between councillors and head office, and all three parties are recognised at the Local Government Association and have their own party groups there. For the purposes of selecting candidates, rules and procedures vary from party to party, with Labour being the most rigid and prescriptive (one year's membership and formal interview required) and the Liberal Democrats being the least (party membership not necessarily a prerequisite).

Composition

In 2005 the Employers' Organisation for local government and the Improvement and Development Agency carried out the third census of local authority councillors in England and Wales, to provide accurate and timely information on the roles and characteristics of local councillors. This census is carried out periodically, the previous one being in 2001, and provides a snapshot of the profile of elected members on district, unitary and county councils in England. On the basis of the information produced from the census, it is possible for local government, central government and representative bodies to assess the impact of policies and initiatives designed to attract a more diverse pool of candidates for local elections.

In 2001, the census found that the average councillor in England was likely to be around fifty-seven years of age, white, male, of public sector background and university educated. Since its election in 1997 the government has introduced a range of policies designed to attract more women, the young and ethnic minority candidates to serve on local councils, including modernising structures and providing annual allowances to compensate for time taken off work. On this occasion, the main findings were as follows:

- 70.3 per cent of councillors were male and 29.1 per cent were female, the remainder not disclosing their gender. This represented an increase in the proportion of female councillors from 27.8 per cent in 1997, although the proportion is still considerably lower than in the adult population as a whole (52.0 per cent).
- The average age of councillors has increased from 55.4 years in 1997 to 56.9 in 2001 and 57.8 in 2004. In 2004, 86.9 per cent of councillors were aged 45 and over, compared to 54.4 per cent of the overall adult population.

- 96.5 per cent of councillors were white and 3.5 per cent came from an ethnic minority background. Significantly higher proportions of the overall adult population were from an ethnic minority background (8.4 per cent).
- The proportion of councillors who were retired increased from 34.1 per cent in 1997 to 38.7 per cent in 2004, compared to 22.5 per cent of the adult population overall.

The census also showed that councillors spend an average of 21.5 hours per week on council and political business. Most councillors were motivated to become a councillor to 'serve the community'. The average length of service of a councillor was 8.3 years. A majority of councillors, 53.6 per cent, held one or more positions of leading responsibility within the council and on average, councillors were members of 3.7 committees. Workwise, 35.5 per cent of councillors were employees and 16.4 per cent were self-employed. Of these councillors, 36.7 per cent were in managerial/executive positions and 28.1 per cent in professional or technical jobs. The majority of councillors in employment worked in the private sector (66.1 per cent). Councillors are significantly higher qualified than the general population – just over half (50.2 per cent) of councillors hold a qualification equivalent to NVQ level 4 and above (i.e. degree, professional qualification); the figure is 22.2 per cent in the population overall.

Representatives' duties

Once elected, there is no legal duty on a councillor to perform surgeries or expedite casework on behalf of their constituents. The vast majority of councils have a system in place to facilitate this but a handful do not. However, if a councillor wishes to secure re-election then their ward duties are crucial. Similarly, once on the council, by law the minimum commitment is to sit on the full council and the Overview and Scrutiny Committee and to attend at least one council meeting every six months. Unless the full council grants a leave of absence (e.g. for medical reasons) then a councillor will be deemed to have resigned and a by-election automatically called (unless elections are due in six months or less) if they do not meet this requirement.

Since 2000, each councillor has received a modest annual taxable allowance to enable them to carry out their representative duties and offset losses to earnings etc. Prior to this, the only allowances available were in the form of allowances per meeting attended, which was deemed to make local government only viable for those retired, unemployed or without work and family responsibilities (see composition above). As part of the drive to modernise and improve local democracy, the new allowances and pensions scheme for councillors was ushered in. The flat rate allowance for each councillor, subject to statutory limits, is set by each council annually on the basis of recommendations made by an independent locally recruited panel. The basic allowance can vary hugely between authorities, depending on the type and character of the authority, with some councils continuing to view the scheme with suspicion and setting lower than average allowances. Additional allowances are available for those with special responsibilities, such as sitting on the council's executive or chairing a committee. Meetings allowances are also available for those sitting on national or regional local government bodies, but these are not part of the local government scheme or subject to statutory controls and are payable by the body concerned.

The responsibilities of each councillor are determined annually at the full council's annual general meeting, which also convenes immediately after any local elections. Party groups and independents will decide their nominations beforehand and then present these to the full council for a vote. The range of offices contested include:

- mayor and deputy mayor (in non-elected mayoral cities and boroughs);
- chair and vice-chair of full council (in elected mayoral or county and district councils);
- chairs and vice-chairs of quasi-judicial regulatory (i.e. planning and licensing) committees (in district and unitary councils) and Overview and Scrutiny Committee;
- places on the council cabinet/executive, overview and scrutiny committees/panels and regulatory committees;
- other panels and sub-committees.

There are no requirements or qualifications required for any office beyond eligibility to be a councillor, though some may not be held at the same time and rules concerning outside interests remain applicable. Some parties place restrictions on holding some civic offices and party group offices, for instance preventing the chief whip from chairing committees or sitting on the executive. For those not elected to civic office among the opposition group on the council (for those in majority control) there are other roles, such as 'shadowing' the executive or acting as lead spokesperson on a particular issue, but these are at the discretion of the group concerned and have no official status.

Standards

Alongside the allowances scheme, in 2001 the government introduced the Standards Board for England and its accompanying regime. The creation of the Standards Board and the regime it oversees was in response to recent local government corruption scandals and the overall drive towards improving standards in public life. The Standards Board acts as the central agency to enforce the local government code of conduct, which all councillors must sign and is legally enforceable by the board. Each council must adopt and modify (within limits) the model code published by Parliament in 2001. The code covers not only principal authorities but also parish and town councils, the Greater London Authority, national parks authorities, fire and police authorities and passenger transport authorities. The board receives complaints made by either members of the public or other councillors and decides on the basis of the investigation by its ethical standards officers whether or not to refer the matter to the Adjudication Panel for England, the body set up to rule on complaints under the supervision of the Department for Constitutional Affairs. The panel's tribunals hear and rule on both cases and appeals and may issue sanctions against councillors found in breach of the code of conduct, ranging from censure to full removal from office and/or prevention from standing for election for a defined period. The Standards Board has been the target of repeated criticism that the standards regime itself is now being abused to further petty endeavours and that it investigates and rules on complaints too slowly.

The Local Government Act 2000

The system of decision making that underpinned the working of local government from 1835 for the next 165 years was that of the committee system, whereby councillors sat on a committee-by-committee basis to determine the policies of the council via a constant cycle of meetings. The committee system was already suggested for reform by the Redcliffe-Maud Royal Commission in

1969 but the impetus for the introduction of a new system did not lead to more a concrete blueprint until almost thirty years later. Having entered government in 1997 with a firm commitment to the introduction of elected mayors (muted among some in the party to the choice of having an elected mayor) after a trial, in the form of the relatively painless referendum, yet painful introduction of an elected mayor for London in the form of the GLA, Labour's manifesto commitment came to pass in the landmark Local Government Act 2000, which enables the introduction of elected mayors, streamlined governance arrangements in most local authorities, councillors' allowances and the standards regime. It also gives effect to the duty to promote the 'economic, social and environmental wellbeing' of each locality and produce a community strategy to outline its intentions with regard to this.

Under the Act, each council must agree an allowances scheme and ratify the model code of conduct. Furthermore, for the first time ever, each council most codify its governance arrangements in a council constitution, the core document for its activities as a local authority. In 2001, all local authorities were obliged to consult local residents on their governance arrangements in order to ascertain demand for a directly elected mayoral system. That year, sixteen local councils in England held referendums on the question of whether or not to introduce an elected mayor (six on October 18) but only twelve councils have introduced elected mayors as their preferred system of constitution in the thirty-five polls held between 2001 and 2006 (the last being Torbay in 2005). The legislation still permits local residents to petition the council (5 per cent or more required to trigger a referendum) to hold a vote on the question. The results of the votes held so far are shown in Table 3.3.

Table 3.3: Mayoral referendum results

Local authority	Date	Yes votes	Yes vote %	No votes	No vote %	Turnout %
Berwick-upon-Tweed	7 June 2001	3,617	26	10,212	74	64
Cheltenham	28 June 2001	8,083	33	16,602	67	32
Gloucester	28 June 2001	7,731	32	16,317	68	31
Watford	12 July 2001	7,636	52	7,140	48	25
Doncaster	20 September 2001	35,453	65	19,398	35	25
Kirklees	4 October 2001	10,169	27	27,977	73	13
Sunderland	11 October 2001	9,375	43	12,209	57	10
Brighton & Hove	18 October 2001	22,724	38	37,214	62	32
Hartlepool	18 October 2001	10,667	51	10,294	49	34
Lewisham	18 October 2001	16,822	51	15,914	49	18
Middlesbrough	18 October 2001	29,067	84	5,422	16	34
North Tyneside	18 October 2001	30,262	58	22,296	42	36
Sedgefield	18 October 2001	10,628	47	11,869	53	33
Redditch	8 November 2001	7,250	44	9,198	56	28
Durham	20 November 2001	8,327	41	11,974	59	29
Harrow	6 December 2001	17,502	43	23,554	57	26
Harlow	24 January 2002	5,296	25	15,490	75	25
Plymouth	24 January 2002	29,559	41	42,811	59	40
Newham	31 January 2002	27,263	68	12,687	32	26
Shepway	31 January 2002	11,357	44	14,438	56	36
Southwark	31 January 2002	6,054	31	13,217	69	11
West Devon	31 January 2002	3,555	23	12,190	77	42
Bedford	21 February 2002	11,316	67	5,537	33	16
Hackney	2 May 2002	24,697	59	10,547	41	32
Mansfield	2 May 2002	8,973	55	7,350	45	21
Newcastle-under-Lyme	2 May 2002	12,912	44	16,468	56	32
Oxford	2 May 2002	14,692	44	18,686	56	34
Stoke on Trent	2 May 2002	28,601	58	20,578	42	27
Corby	1 October 2002	5,351	46	6239	54	31
Ealing	12 December 2002	9,454	45	11,655	55	10
Ceredigion	20 May 2004	5,308	27	14,013	73	36
Isle of Wight	5 May 2005	28,786	44	37,097	56	60
Fenland	14 July 2005	5,509	24	17,296	76	34
Torbay	14 July 2005	18,074	55	14,682	45	32
Crewe and Nantwich	4 May 2006	11,808	39	18,768	61	35

Under the Local Government Act 2000, each council must choose (subject to consultation) its preferred governance arrangements from four models on offer, these being:

- directly elected mayor and cabinet;
- directly elected mayor and council manager;
- leader and cabinet;
- revamped committee system (also known as alternative arrangements/fourth option).

At May 2006 the council constitutions in England were as follows:

Model	Number
Leader and cabinet	314
Revamped committee system	59
Elected mayor and cabinet	12
Elected mayor and council manager	1

The majority of councils opted for the leader-and-cabinet model as that which most closely resembled the conventional pre-2000 leader-and-committee system. The revamped committee system was only available to those (largely rural) district councils with 85,000 or fewer residents or to a council which held a referendum on having an elected mayor and chose this model as their fallback position, of which only Brighton & Hove City Council has done. The mayor-and-council-manager model was only adopted in one council (Stoke-on-Trent) and proposed in only two referendums (the other being Fenland District Council in 2005); it has not caught the popular imagination on account of being so alien to local government traditions, to the point that its abolition has been mooted.

Under the reforms the role of the full council has been reasserted, particularly with regard to passing key strategies by setting the policy framework (the array of annual performance plans and strategies such as community safety, libraries and sports), passing the budget and appointing key officers. Furthermore, a new key duty on local councillors who do not sit on the executive under either of the main models is that of overview and scrutiny. The Overview and Scrutiny Committee, which comprises all councillors not sitting on the executive, examines the council's key decisions (those made under the 'Forward Plan') and also delegates work to themed panels to further scrutinise the actions of the executive. Put simply, scrutiny is the process of reviewing and developing council policies, making proposals to the executive and asking the executive to look again at its decisions. While the role of backbench councillors is clearly defined in the Act, some have refused to accept what they regard as a demotion and as such the concept of scrutiny and its execution is not what it could be. Scrutiny is also undermined by some aspects of party discipline and the culture of local government meetings, though recent efforts on the part of government and some agencies have attempted to address this. On the other hand, some councils have taken to the role and have also undertaken pioneering work in holding other local public agencies to account. Since the Act was passed, councils were also entrusted with a health scrutiny role over the local NHS following the abolition of community health councils.

4 Human resources

The role of the council officer, including legal duties and framework governing relations with councillors. Staffing levels and role of private sector.

The local authority officer has been an abiding feature of local government since the era of the parish clerk. In the post-war period local government emerged as a major employer within the British public sector and remains today its largest component (2.2 million workers to the civil service's 0.5 million). Local government staff range from street sweepers to chief executives, with, *inter alia*, teachers, social workers and planning officers in between. Much of the well-known traditional nomenclature – county treasurers, borough solicitors and town clerks, for instance – has been replaced with either legally designated posts or more modern titles. Similarly, the drive towards efficiency and more joined-up services has seen senior posts merged, with many directors of education becoming directors of children's services, for instance. Beneath the senior management tier is an array of specialist staff, such as planners, policy officers, lawyers and personnel staff. The integral role of officers in carrying out the day-to-day business of the local authority, quite often under delegated powers, should not be under-estimated. Though trust is required in any relationship of this nature, ultimately accountability is defined by performance as officers remain answerable to councillors for their conduct.

Table 4.1: Local government employees by type

| | Male | | Female | | |
	Full-time	Part-time	Full-time	Part-time	Total
Counties	109,477	43,331	208,843	401,315	762,966
Metropolitan authorities	115,044	29,529	172,577	226,864	544,014
English unitaries	73,570	24,176	104,551	174,655	376,952
London boroughs	59,583	12,763	89,813	88,463	250,622
Welsh unitaries	36,688	11,254	47,542	69,415	164,899
Shire districts	57,191	10,865	40,373	34,214	142,643
Total	451,553	131,918	663,699	994,926	2,242,096

June 2005 figures

Member–officer relations

The interface between members and officers in British local government has historically been defined by deference to elected mandate and the respect for impartial advice. Member–officer relations have evolved since both the Bains report in 1972 and the Widdicombe report in 1986, not least because of the changes ushered in under the Local Government Act 2000 which have seen councillors' roles and the decision-making process modernised and ultimately altered. The evolution continues, however, as the role of local government continues to change. Ultimately, it could be said that the relationship that matters most is that between the leader of the council and the chief executive, as the accountable public front for the member–officer interface on an authority-wide level. Aside from the senior posts designated under law and the framework by which officers are appointed and interact with councillors within the decision-making process, the interface can vary from authority to authority, with some councils being regarded as 'officer led' in terms of the dynamic between councillors and staff, and this continues to exercise academic minds. While political debate can lead to heated exchanges, the provision of advice to councillors and the response from councillors should (in theory) be devoid of any animosity. Guidance and common sense dictate that professional courtesy and the avoidance of any familiarity between councillors and officers should underpin their dealings. However, under the recent changes, the closeness at which executive members and scrutiny chairs will encounter their support staff and the relevant directorate officers means that this barrier has to some extent been eliminated. Similarly, the frontline role envisaged for backbench councillors means that increased interaction will take place between them and staff in neighbourhood offices. Nonetheless, theoretical political impartiality from officers demands that councillors themselves should not be seen to interfere in the direct running of services beyond their civic office or ward representative role.

The legal framework

Unlike other countries, there is no organised local civil service in the UK. Local government officers enjoy some degree of national organisation and a professional framework but contracts and careers are a matter for each council to decide. The system is also based around, for the most part, single career paths by professionals; there are no generalist local government officers who change departments periodically. While contractual matters will remain a matter for each local authority to decided, the government has consulted on introducing a code of conduct for local government employees in the near future (*Standards of Conduct in English Local Government: The Future*, published by the Office of the Deputy Prime Minister in December 2005).

Under the Local Government Act 2000, each local authority is required (depending on type) to appoint five statutory officers and to recognise their role within the council constitution, these being:

- head of paid service
- monitoring officer
- chief financial officer
- director of social services
- chief education officer.

While the posts are laid down in law, their job titles are not and most commonly the head of paid service is known as the chief executive (or in some cases managing director), with the monitoring officer and the chief financial officer often known respectively as the director or head of law or legal services and finance or financial services, depending on the authority. District authorities are not required to appoint education or social services officers as they do not provide these services but counties, unitaries and metropolitan authorities must. All tiers must appoint to the first three core posts.

Within the context of the Act, councillors must accept the advice given by the three core posts regardless of political or personal judgement on their part. In particular, the monitoring officer is empowered and required to ensure that the authority's actions remain legal and never *ultra vires* at all times.

Concern over 'twin-tracking' (the trend among some senior officers to pursue political careers on other councils) and its attendant effect of politicising local authority management led the Conservative government to charge the Widdicombe Review (the Inquiry into the Conduct of Local Authority Business) with finding a method of preventing this. The government responded to its recommendations (*The Conduct of Local Authority Business*) by legislating for the Local Government and Housing Act 1989, which introduced for the first time the principle of politically restricted posts. The Act also created the designated post of political assistant for party groups, a researcher and policy officer who would enable councillors to receive political advice. The effect of political restriction is to prevent staff regarded as holding politically restricted posts from standing for election at any level (or being employed if already holding office), campaigning on behalf of others in an election (including speaking to the media) or holding any elected office within a political party. While breaching political restriction would be regarded as a disciplinary matter for the employee, the council's monitoring officer is required to ensure its staff comply with the legislation. The following posts are regarded as automatically politically restricted:

- head of paid service
- statutory chief officers
- deputy chief officers
- monitoring officer
- chief finance officer
- officers with delegated powers
- political assistants.

The Act and its accompanying secondary legislation also regard all council officers above spinal column point 44 (£33,984 in 2005) on the local government pay scale as being politically restricted. Such officers are, however, allowed to appeal to an independent adjudicator if they are of the view that their post is not 'politically sensitive'. The Office of the Deputy Prime Minister's paper *Standards of Conduct in English Local Government: The Future*, while retaining the principle of political restriction, suggested that only the most senior and sensitive posts should be subject to it and that appeals should be handled by local standards committees rather than the independent adjudicator.

Local government professions

The Local Government Employers (LGE) organisation was created in 2006 following the review undertaken of the former Employers' Organisation (EO) and the Improvement and Development Agency (IDeA). Under the new arrangements, many of the former EO's policy roles have transferred to the IDeA, with LGE acting on behalf of all English councils as the national body for pay bargaining and employment conditions in negotiations with staff and central government. Pay scales (with spinal column points and grades) are determined by this body, which are then used by each council to determine the salaries for its officer posts. Some occupations come under specialist categories for pay negotiations at LGE, namely:

- blind workshops' employees
- chief executives and chief officers
- coroners
- craftworkers
- doctors assisting local authorities
- education (independent and non-LEA)
- principal fire officers
- fire and rescue services
- forensic medical examiners
- local government services
- police
- youth and community workers.

The National Joint Council (NJC) determines the pay and conditions of some 1.4 million local government officers. In 1997, the NJC agreed the Single Status Agreement, which ended the divide in negotiations between blue- and white-collar workers, with particular reference to the pay divide by gender. Implementation of single status has proven costly to many councils, not least because of the question of backdated claims for equal pay being awarded.

Unlike the civil service and other countries' local governments, there is no centralised system for graduate entry into local government or a fast-track career system. However, the National Graduate Development Programme was established by the EO to make local government a viable and attractive career for new graduates as part of the drive to modernise and improve the calibre of those in the professions. The scheme, which continues today, involves a two-year traineeship hosted by a local authority on behalf of the programme, which recruits biannually and is limited in number. It also offers participants a post-graduate diploma and at the end of the two years a likely job offer.

Local government staff are eligible to join the Local Government Pension Scheme, which covers all councils and also bodies admitted to the scheme on the basis of their association with local government. However, recent changes to the so-called 85-year rule (which allows those whose age and continuous employment in local government add up to 85) has seen the age at which local government employees can retire raised, much to the annoyance of trade unions.

Outsourcing

Under compulsory competitive tendering (CCT) and then Best Value, many local government services and therefore service providers, in the form of staff, have been outsourced to private firms and other organisations. This process first began with the awarding of contracts for routine tasks such as grounds maintenance, refuse collection and school meals ('blue-collar CCT') to either external providers or in-house bids (direct labour organisations) and was later extended via 'white-collar CCT' to areas such as IT support and housing benefit administration. Under Best Value, all local government services must be considered for rigorous assessment of the potential savings gained via outsourcing; this includes areas such as corporate communications, catering and personnel.

When council staff are transferred into new organisations on the basis of outsourcing, regulations take effect to protect their conditions of employment (including pensions). The most recent regulations, which replace previous longstanding arrangements, are set out in the Transfer of Undertakings (Protection of Employment) Regulations 2006.

5 National framework

Relations between central and local government, auditing and inspection regimes and the role of national umbrella organisations. Publicity code.

The recent history of local government in the UK is one of often excessive central government intervention. Crystallised in Anthony Crosland's 'the party's over' speech to amassed councillors in 1976, the prevailing attitude of central government ever since has been that local government tends to be wasteful and at odds with the worldview of the governing party nationally, never more so than at the nadir reached in the standoff between Margaret Thatcher and the new urban left during the 1980s. While it may be fashionable to speak of the 'dark days' of Thatcherism, the trend began under Labour, ever the unrepentant centralists. This analysis places emphasis on political behaviour when, in fact, in a not entirely coincidental explanation, local government continues to exist according to the parameters set by central government in the form of the sovereign Parliament, of which it is a 'creature'. Since the 'dark days' of the Conservative administrations, the watchwords have often been 'partnership' and 'earned autonomy', with specific policies aimed at reassuring (never successfully) that those days are over. While Labour has abolished universal capping, it did retain, and subsequently use, reserve powers to cap individual local authorities where it saw fit. Rather than the next set of local elections, local councils are most likely to ponder the outcome of decisions made in Whitehall under the next spending review. As such, a word should be said on the gearing effect of the gradual transition from locally raised finance to almost outright dependency on central government grants and the increasing use of ring-fencing.

The decision of Labour in 1997 to ratify the European Charter of Local Self-Government, an act which its Eurosceptic (but almost sincere in comparison) predecessor had refused to do, positively rings hollow if one considers its prescriptions around local financial autonomy and protection from central interference. In spite of this, Labour has repeatedly banged the drum of 'earned autonomy', whereby the best-performing councils should receive adequate freedoms to reward their performance, while the worst offenders should be singled out for intervention. The mechanism used to identify the best- and worst-performing councils is called comprehensive performance assessment (CPA) (see Chapter 1). Though its opponents are wont to cite the ballot box as the ultimate method of achieving the desired leadership and accountability over poor performance, CPA was intended to provide a benchmarkable standard from which voters could base their political decisions. As ever, the devil is in the detail and the 'Audit and Inspection Regimes' section below will discuss how this has worked in practice as the definitive *leitmotiv* for New Labour's approach to central–local relations. Another tangible example of New Labour's approach to central–local relations was the schools funding crisis of 2003, where, in the war of words between the Department for Education and Skills and the Local Government Association (LGA) over the shortfall in LEA budgets, central government alleged the issue to be the product of local mismanagement of increased funding. These flashpoints aside, one only has to look at the legislation of recent reforms and their stated rationale to detect and document the trend towards centralisation. Essentially, New Labour has formalised and sought to legitimise the naked centralism of its predecessor.

Central–local relations

When New Labour entered government in 1997, its watchword was 'partnership', nowhere more so than in relation to local government. Regardless of tangible examples of this arrangement being breached, this section will consider the formal arrangements between central and local government established since 1997. On a daily basis, the lead department of state for local government issues, from policy to operational and financial decisions, is the Department for Communities and Local Government (DCLG – the fourth such department since 1997), which was created in May 2006. In November 1997, the deputy Prime Minister, John Prescott, and the chair of the LGA, Jeremy Beecham, signed *A Framework for Partnership*, an accord which established the Central–Local Partnership (CLP) and outlined how the two bodies envisaged central–local relations developing under the new government, including an acknowledgement of mutual dependency and a set of shared objectives. Aside from closer working arrangements, the document committed central government to organise a biannual summit and to give the LGA consultation rights on government policy. The document outlined the framework as being to:

- promote effective local democracy, with strong and accountable political leadership;
- support continuous improvement in the quality of local government services, helping councils to make a real difference for their communities;

- support consideration in partnership of priorities for local government, and the definition of an agreed list of priorities;
- increase the discretion and local accountability of local authorities on expenditure and revenue-raising matters, within such disciplines as are essential to national economic policy;
- enable and encourage local authorities to modernise and revitalise their structures and working practices so as to provide accountable and responsive leadership for local communities;
- as a general principle, provide for services and decision making affecting local communities to be undertaken at the level which is closest to the people and area to be served, consistent with competence, practicality and cost effectiveness;
- uphold standards of conduct in public life, founded on principles of selflessness, integrity, objectivity, accountability, openness, honesty and leadership.

While the DCLG acts as the lead department for local government in England, local councils' work brings them into contact with most other government departments on a daily basis (such as the Home Office on anti-social behaviour, the Department for Transport on transport funding etc.) and this is reflected in the make-up of the CLP. The following departments are also members of the partnership:

- Cabinet Office
- Department for Constitutional Affairs
- Department for Culture, Media and Sport
- Department for Education and Skills
- Department for Environment, Food and Rural Affairs
- Department for Health
- Home Office

- Department for Trade and Industry
- Department for Transport
- Treasury
- Department for Work and Pensions.

Prior to the creation of the CLP, discussions took place in the Consultative Council on Local Government Finance.

Audit and inspection regimes

Local government is supervised on a constant basis by the machinery of central government, with the secretary of state in possession of considerable powers to intervene in the minutest aspects of its operations. This culture extends not only to the operational aspect but increasingly, as part of this culture, to the role of inspection as a tool by which central government is able to direct the activities of local government to its choosing. A plethora of inspectorates, each covering different aspects of local governance, exists at the behest of central government, though even these are not immune from the drive for efficiency and integrated working and as such the regime is also undergoing a series of mergers.

Established in 1982 as part of the Conservative government's drive to achieve stricter finances on the part of local government, the Audit Commission is a non-departmental public body responsible for regulating the finances of local councils, in addition to other local public services such as housing associations, NHS trusts and police and fire and rescue authorities. It appoints a district auditor to each council to act as its liaison point, although through the mainstreaming of the work of the District Audit Service within the commission this post is less important than was previously the case. It should not be confused with the National Audit Office, which is a separate organisation that inspects the finances of central government.

In addition to the Audit Commission, two other inspectorates are closely involved in the inspection regime of local government. The Commission for Social Care Inspection (CSCI) was created in 2004 as the successor to the Social Services Inspectorate and took on some joint work previously undertaken by the Audit Commission. The CSCI is concerned with the social-care role of local councils providing or commissioning these services (county and single-tier) and also the joint work councils undertake with the NHS in this area; it is also concerned with the NHS's private and voluntary sector partners, who undertake an increasing role on behalf of local authorities. The CSCI then issues individual reports on each council's performance in relation to the provision of services for older people, the disabled, those with learning disabilities and people with mental health problems. Since 2005 it has worked with other inspectorates to provide joint area reviews of children's services. Another key inspectorate, especially in relation to the latter, is the Office for Standards in Education, more commonly known as Ofsted. Ofsted was created in 1993 as the chief agency for the inspection of schools, the post of Her Majesty's Chief Inspector (and the more numerous Her Majesty's Inspectors) having existed since the creation of formal public education in the nineteenth century. Since its inception the powers of Ofsted have steadily increased, with the inclusion of post-sixteen education and childcare in recent years. In addition to providing five-yearly reports on the performance of every school, the agency is also responsible for the direction of failing schools under the special measures regime.

A major component of the Audit Commission's work with local government is comprehensive performance assessment. CPA was first floated in the 2001 White Paper *Strong Local Leadership,*

Quality Public Services and was rolled out to county and single-tier councils in 2002, with districts coming on stream via a less rigid assessment model in 2003. The regime was also placed on a statutory footing in the Local Government Act 2003 after a series of legal challenges by local councils on the basis of the poor grades they were awarded after inspection. The original scheme used performance data from an array of inspectorates to provide a central score in the form of a corporate assessment for each council's performance across its services which then placed it in a category-based national league table:

Total score	2 or 3	4	5	6	7 or 8
Category	Poor	Weak	Fair	Good	Excellent

Those councils securing an excellent score were promised enhanced freedoms and flexibilities in reward of their performance, including:

- reductions in capital and revenue ring-fencing;
- reductions in inspection;
- exemption from certain statutory plan requirements;
- the power to trade;
- membership of the Innovation Forum.

The councils ranked lowest in the 'poor' category were then regarded as candidates for intervention, though the 'basket cases' were already known by that point. As we have seen, critics of the regime have claimed that local accountability is best maintained through the ballot box at local elections, though some councils have claimed the process has given them the opportunity to focus and better themselves. As it involves a visit by a team of inspectors, the process can be as psychologically gruelling for a council as an Ofsted inspection is for schools. Under the regime, the worst councils are subject to intervention measures, first in the form of an improvement plan but also including the power of the secretary of state to demand that the authority seek external support or contract out its services to another provider. Critics also argue that the freedoms and flexibilities envisaged for the strongest performers have failed to materialise. In 2005 the Audit Commission published its evaluation of the regime and proposals for reform, in the form of the 'Harder Test' that will make obtaining higher scores harder than in previous assessments. The new system will involve instead a star ratings system of four stars (the highest) through to no stars to allow councils and voters to judge their authority's performance. The regime is in place until 2008, after which its future looks very much uncertain, with some form of less rigid self-assessment more than likely to replace it.

Representing local government

Principal local authorities in England and Wales are represented by one single organisation, the Local Government Association (LGA). The LGA was formed in April 1997 from the merger of the three separate tier-based associations: the Association of County Councils, the Association of District Councils and the Association of Metropolitan Authorities. The merger was based on the fact that English local authorities had one year previously begun to exist on a unitary pattern in urban areas with the traditional two-tier system retained for rural areas and as such the retention of three separate associations would not serve these authorities as well as one single organisation could. The LGA speaks as the single voice for English councils (a separate entity also exists for Wales) but one or two authorities have seceded from the organisation over the question of membership fees. It also represents police and fire authorities and passenger transport authorities, as well as national parks authorities. Non-principal authorities such as parish and town councils are represented by the National Association of Local Councils, which was set up in 1947. Besides its provision of policy guidance to local councils and its formal role within the Central–Local Partnership, the LGA sees itself as the lobbying arm of local government to both central government and Parliament. In addition, it has taken on itself to promote the reputation of local government as part of its drive to enhance the status of local government and bid for more powers, recognising the poor estimation in which local government is held in some quarters that makes centralisation easier to achieve. As a membership organisation, it elects office holders annually and organises on a party group basis according to the allocation of councillors in England and Wales. After several years of being led by Labour, it is now led by the Conservative group, though the organisation works on the basis of consensus between groups rather than outright partisanship and quite often its policy line draws agreement across the two main groups. The association contains a number of formally recognised and constituted special interest groups, such as the County Councils Network and groups for metropolitan and unitary councils (effectively continuing the work of the predecessor organisations), as well as passenger transport authorities and police authorities. Special interest groups also exist for coastal local authorities and those using alternative governance arrangements. Several regional associations exist, including the Association of London Government (ALG). The ALG is unique in comparison to other regions in that it actually discharges several functions in Greater London in relation to the London Housing Board as well as the parking appeals service for the capital.

The Improvement and Development Agency (IDeA) was established in 1999 as a successor to the Local Government Management Board (the other being the Employers' Organisation), with an emphasis on modernisation and improvement. Its role is more attuned to policy guidance and the provision of tailored consultancy and training for local councils around these areas, as well its formal role in the beacon councils scheme and peer reviews. It is a sister organisation of the LGA, regarded as part of the 'LGA family' but with a distinct organisational identity. In 1999, the Employers' Organisation for local government (EO) was also formed to act as the representative arm of English local government in national pay bargaining. However, a recent review of the EO's activities recommended the creation of a new and more focused organisation, Local Government Employers (LGE), which became live in 2006, and several of the EO's policy functions passed to the IDeA. The other organisations of the LGA family include the Local Authorities Coordinators of Regulatory Services (LACORS), which serves local councils responsible for trading and food safety standards, the Local Authorities Research and Intelligence Association (LARIA), which advises on best practice in research, and the Local Government International Bureau (LGIB), which supports local councils' international work as well as organising the formal role in European institutions of the Committee of the Regions. LACORS, LARIA and LGIB all predate the LGA's formation. The funding of the LGA family comes mainly from the top slice of central government grant, membership subscriptions and revenue-raising activities such as consultancy, publications and conferences.

Separate arrangements exist for Wales within the LGA in the form of the Welsh Local Government Association, which has increasingly moved towards outright independence following devolution to Wales and the recent reviews of public services in the principality.

o far even for Thatcher's Conservative Party before it defenestrated er later that year. After the pitched ideological battles of the hatcher and Major administrations and following the brief period f 'partnership' between the Labour government and the Labour-led Local Government Association, the approach of central government as been to lay down a framework that leaves local councils with no hoice other than to run their finances in a prudent and cost-effective manner. Similarly, gestures such as the abolition of universal capping (whereby each council knew upfront how much they could raise their council tax by to fund their budget requirement) were coupled with the retention of capping powers vested in the secretary of state, which have been used when deemed necessary. Under the unwritten constitution, political expediency demands nothing less. The current government has attempted to lessen the scope for contention by moving to a three-yearly system of budgeting its spending on local authorities in order to allow for better planning locally but also stave off the annual round of representations to seek a better allocation for each local authority.

In terms of raw figures, local government spending, estimated at £119.5 billion in 2003/4, represented just over a quarter of all public spending in the UK and 11 per cent of national income. It is worth noting the work of the Lyons inquiry at this point. The inquiry, led by Michael Lyons, a former local authority chief executive turned government fixer, was established in June 2004 to continue the work undertaken by the Balance of Funding Review, another inquiry which had been chaired by the then local government minister, Nick Raynsford, but subsequently kicked into the long grass when it failed to decisively recommend an alternative to the status quo. Local government taxation, in the form of the current council tax, is particularly loathed as a highly visible and transparent charge, as opposed to being absorbed into general taxation deducted at source.

Scotland has long had its own association in the form of the Confederation of Scottish Local Authorities, which represents its thirty-two local councils and exists largely on the same lines as its English equivalent in terms of its role. Northern Ireland's twenty-six district councils had long refused to fully co-operate for a variety of historic reasons but in 2001 came together to launch the Northern Ireland Local Government Association. The association campaigned against the outcome of the Review of Public Administration in the province, which saw the government accept the recommendation to reduce the number of councils to seven, largely achieving cross-community backing for its opposition to the proposals.

Publicity Code

Local authority publicity can sometimes be controversial, par-ticularly concerning the use of public money to fund what can be seen as political advertising. The current regime, enforced under the Code of Recommended Practice on Local Authority Publicity, introduced in 1986 and amended in 2001, was very much a product of the fraught state of relations between central and local govern-ment during the pitched ideological skirmishes of that era. The code makes it clear that councils are entitled and expected to promote their activities to local electorates in order to reinforce local accountability. It accepts that councils do business in a political environment but they should refrain from using council publicity for political purposes. Electoral law, most notably the Representation of the People Act 1983, makes provision for the neutral conduct of council communications departments during election periods (the so-called 'purdah'), whereby it is forbidden to even allow existing councillors in positions of responsibility access to council resources in this regard. Separate arrangements exist under the Local

Government Act 2000 concerning the publicity required during the staging of mayoral referendums, with councils expected to present the case for and against in a neutral manner.

6   Local governmer finance

History of local government finance and outline of system, including grants (also EU funding) and cou Also private finance initiative, efficiency review, Bes local area agreements, business improvement districts government.

By reputation alone, local government finance represents tedious aspect of its existence. It is also the most contentiou been behind political headlines for decades. No other extends its influence into the minutest aspect of local gov operations, from a single paperclip in a school to a chief exe salary. Ever since Anthony Crosland's already much-discuss party's over' speech in 1976, local authority finance has the forefront of all debates about the future of local governn the UK. Local government then weathered several storms, fro introduction of capping and the poll tax under Margaret Th to the schools budget crisis of 2003 under Tony Blair. No government issue before or since has inspired a disturbance of scale of the poll tax riot in London in 1990, not to mentior defiance on the part of some councillors which saw them jailec non-payment of the hated local tax, which ultimately proved a

The inquiry's remit in June 2004 was primarily financial but in September 2005 it was widened to include the form and function of English local government, with an extended timeframe to report by the end of 2006, therefore placing its recommendations beyond the May 2005 general election. Since then, the inquiry has published a series of interim reports outlining its thinking and approach to determining the future for both local government finance and local government itself. However, critics argued that Lyons's work would be effectively undermined by developments taking place elsewhere, such as the long-awaited local government White Paper and the removal of education finance from local government's sphere of influence, as the inquiry's remit had fallen out of sync with the policy-making cycle. The second interim report, in May 2006, argued that central government had to permit local authorities more freedom to 'place shape' by supervising their activities less, but local government at the same time should raise its game by providing better political leadership. On the question of finance, he hinted at recommendations around more service charges, such as a recycling levy for those who fail to recycle their domestic waste and a hotel bed tax. However, at the time of writing, it would appear that both Lyons and the government favour some form of reformed council tax rather than any radical solution, having effectively ruled out a local income tax. This may present itself again as a generational question, as the current government does not want to be seen as being the one to replace one hated tax with another.

Local government funding

The standard spending assessment continues to be the most important aspect of local government finance in terms of assessing local need and reflecting this in the annual settlement provided to each council, calculating the revenue support grant (RSG) allocation and the capping limit. The RSG for each local authority is calculated to fund local council services by central government and allocated using the formula spending share system, which ascertains local circumstances and the ability of councils to match spending with the available tax-raising capacity. As such, an authority with higher spending needs but a lower tax yield on account of local income would receive an adjusted RSG, which is claimed to be to the disadvantage of more affluent areas, forcing these councils to raise council tax to cope with the shortfall. The displacement between grant and taxation is known as gearing, namely the ratio of grant to tax. As the local government finance settlement has increased, the scope for local taxation increases has lessened, and council tax now constitutes only around 20 per cent of local authority spending. Within the central government allocation for local government, grants are also split between capital and revenue spending. Capital spending relates to the acquisition and maintenance of assets (buildings etc.) by the local authority, while revenue spending is mostly concerned with salaries. Both categories are subject to separate accounts; for instance, capital receipts from the sale of assets cannot be used to fund revenue-related activities. Those councils which provide housing services are also required to maintain a separate housing revenue account (HRA) relating to their spending and revenue raising from the provision of housing, with HRA subsidy available to some authorities in order to finance this. Since the introduction of the ring-fenced dedicated schools grant in 2006, the funding made available to LEAs as part of the central government grant has been reduced to make allowance for direct funding to schools, a further erosion of local financial autonomy some argue.

EU funding

The European Union provides funds to regenerate the economies of the poorest regions of the twenty-five member states. While the UK is economically one of the richest member states, several regions do qualify for EU funding under the criteria set. The criteria are known as Objectives 1, 2 and 3, with 1 representing the highest level of need for spending. The European Regional Development Fund makes finance available for projects in those designated regions, with the counties of Cornwall (South West region), Merseyside (North West) and South Yorkshire (Yorkshire and the Humber) being eligible for Objective 1. All other regions qualify for Objective 2 and 3 funding. The European Social Fund also provides work-related funds across the regions.

In addition to these, the European Structural Fund provides finance for four community initiatives in the UK, with a total spend of £916m over the period 2000–6. These include INTERREG III, to promote inter-regional development and transnational co-operation on spatial development, and URBAN II, to regenerate cities. Both are administered by the Department for Communities and Local Government. Local government, along with government offices, are key agents for delivering on all EU-funded projects in the UK.

Council tax

The council tax had something of a troubled birth and its existence ever since has often been called into question by politicians of all parties. The perennial question remains, however: what to replace it with? Since the inquiry into local government funding is ongoing at the time of publication and any reform would still probably take years to implement, it is best to concentrate on givens. Introduced in 1993 as the successor to the unpopular community charge, the council tax is payable by local residents to their local authority regardless of citizenship or home ownership. The tax is based on the commercial value of residential property, with each property rated within a band according to its 1991 value, with the bands running from A (lowest) to H (highest). Property values (including new build) are assessed by the Valuation Office Agency, an executive agency of HM Revenue and Customs. The council's annual budget must set the Band D for the area on the basis of two adults living in the property, with other bands being automatically set on the basis of this (Band A paying two-thirds of this, Band H twice as much). Single adults living alone are eligible for a 25 per cent discount and the registered unemployed or those on low incomes are entitled to a rebate in the form of council tax benefit.

The bands are as follows (England only):

Band	Value
A	Up to £40,000
B	£40,001 to £52,000
C	£52,001 to £68,000
D	£68,001 to £88,000
E	£88,001 to £120,000
F	£120,001 to £160,000
G	£160,001 to £320,000
H	£320,001 and above

Under the Local Government Finance Act 1992, which introduced the tax (as amended by the Local Government Act 2003), a revaluation of the bands was due to take place in 2005, to take effect in 2007. In September 2005, the government announced that the revaluation would be deferred until after the outcome of the inquiry on local government finance. A similar revaluation for Wales went ahead but saw many properties moved up one or two bands, and the political fallout of such a move in an election year in England was too much to bear.

Council tax directly funds the services of the billing authority, either a unitary or district council. Principal authorities such as counties must levy a precept for their services on the (district) billing authorities beneath them and this is shown as a separate component of the council tax bill. Other entities able to precept billing authorities include the Greater London Authority, police authorities, fire and rescue authorities, and national parks authorities. Parish and town councils also levy a precept for the supplementary services they provide.

In Scotland there is a separate precept for the services provided by Scottish Water, which remains in public ownership. The twenty-six current district councils in Northern Ireland continue to levy rates as their form of local taxation, as existed on the mainland before the introduction of the community charge in 1990.

Capping

The capping of local authority budgets, introduced by the Rates Act 1984, was emblematic of the Tory government's view of local government spending. With the Local Government Act 1999, the government abolished universal capping but retained reserve powers for the secretary of state to intervene in each local authority's budget if he or she considered the stated rise in council tax to be excessive. In 2004, it used the reserve powers for the first time to cap the council tax/precept rises of six local authorities and one fire authority. In 2005, it again used its power to cap the budgets set by seven district councils and once again in 2006 used them to cap the budgets of two unitary authorities. The reason for using the powers to cap 'excessive' (i.e. above single figures) rises is that the government claims it has increased the local government grant year on year and the local authorities, in breach of its prudential-financing principles, are failing to keep their house in order.

Business rates

The nationally administered uniform business rate was also introduced in 1990 as a replacement for the locally set business rates alongside the community charge. However, it was not reformed alongside the community charge and remains in place today. The rate is set by central government and collected locally, though then processed centrally before being redistributed to councils in grant form. The five-yearly revaluation of commercial property is also carried out by the Valuation Office Agency.

The uniform business rate for England is calculated annually (according to the Retail Price Index) by what is known as the 'multiplier'. The multiplier for 2006/7 is 43 pence in the pound, so on a rateable value for a business property of £22,000, the multiplier would represent 22,000 x 0.43 = £9,460. Small businesses and charitable organisations are eligible for relief from business rates.

The system has been criticised as unfair by local councils since its inception on the grounds that they are prevented from either setting the local rate or receiving their fare share back from central government. Labour entered government in 1997 with a promise to return the power to councils to set their own business rates but has not moved on this since and has left it to the Lyons inquiry to determine.

Private finance – PFI and PPP

The diminishing divide between the public and private sector has become an accepted facet of public policy by all three main parties. The two distinct methods of securing private sector capital to fund public projects have become known as private finance initiatives (PFIs) and public–private partnerships (PPPs). Though the two terms are often used interchangeably, this is inaccurate as they describe different forms of public and private sector involvement in a project. The ostensible difference between the two is that in a PFI the private sector takes on an agreed liability to finance a project, while under a PPP the public sector is given an equity share in the venture. PFIs include school-building projects, while an example of a PPP is the London Underground modernisation programme. The most common form of PFI is the design-build-finance-operate (DBFO) schemes, whereby the contract states that the private sector will carry out these four tasks on behalf of the contracting authority. Given both Conservative and Labour support for their retention, private finance is likely to remain a stable form of funding local government capital projects and is effectively beyond contention within the mainstream of both parties.

Efficiency

In August 2003 Peter Gershon, the head of the Office of Government Commerce, was asked by the government to undertake a review of public sector efficiency. This focused on the government's key objective to release resources to fund the frontline services that meet the public's highest priorities by improving the efficiency of service delivery, particularly through the sharing of 'back office' functions (such as co-operating with neighbouring authorities on human resources) and smarter procurement (e.g. entering into joint arrangements with neighbouring authorities or other non-local government public bodies). Gershon published his report in July 2004. The report identified the opportunity to make £21.5 billion of sustainable efficiency gains across the public sector in 2007/8. Of this total, at least £6.45 billion would be achieved by local government in England; equivalent to 7.5 per cent of its 2004/5 baseline expenditure. This figure has been adopted as the official target for local government and it will be met by activities undertaken by councils (comprising nearly half the £6.45 billion target), schools (comprising nearly 40 per cent of the target) and police and fire authorities (comprising about 15 per cent of the target).

The 2004 spending review identified annual savings of 2.5 per cent that could be achieved by local councils. All local authorities must now produce two annual efficiency statements, the 'forward look' (projected savings in the forthcoming year) and the 'backward look' (an assessment of savings achieved and how). Gershon is now very much part of the local government landscape.

Best Value

Introduced as the successor to compulsory competitive tendering in 1999, Best Value provides a framework for the planning, delivery and continuous improvement of services in all principal authorities and others designated 'Best Value authorities'. Best Value is the notion that councils as providers of services to the local community owe it to service users and taxpayers to secure the best value for money available. According to the Local Government Act 1999, all councils must review their activities, applying the 'four Cs' criteria to all council services. These are to:

- challenge why and how the service is provided;
- compare performance with others, including other available providers;
- consult local service users;
- compete on a fair basis to ensure the best service possible.

This is undertaken via Best Value reviews of each council function and the production of a Best Value plan. The Audit Commission also uses Best Value data in its inspection work of each local authority. Local government staff subject to outsourcing of services under Best Value are subject to the provisions of the Transfer of Undertakings (Protection of Employment) legislation.

Local area agreements

A local area agreement (LAA) is a three-year agreement, based on local sustainable community strategies, that sets out the priorities for a local area agreed between central government, represented by the relevant government office, and a locality, represented by the local authority and other strategic partners through their local strategic partnership (see Chapter 9).

LAAs are structured around four policy areas: children and young people, safer and stronger communities, healthier communities and older people, and economic development and enterprise. Their aim is to achieve local goals while also contributing to national priorities and the achievement of standards set by central government. LAAs seek to:

- provide intelligent and mature discussion between local and central government, based on a clear framework and shared understanding of national and local priorities;
- improve local performance, by allowing a more flexible use of

resources, to achieve better outcomes and devolve responsibility;
- enhance efficiency by rationalising non-mainstream funding and reduce bureaucracy to help local partners to join up and enhance community leadership.

Business improvement districts

The Local Government Act 2003 created a new form of local governance, business improvement districts (BIDs), covering recognised business districts within local authorities. Subject to approval by a ballot of local business ratepayers, BIDs may be created in order to secure local environmental improvements paid for by a levy on local businesses. BIDs may only be created at the behest of billing authorities, though the secretary of state may direct their creation over local authority boundaries or veto their creation.

E-government

In 2000 the government set the ambitious target that by December 2005 all councils should be fully e-enabled to allow for the delivery as many services as practicable online. For the first few years the target seemed unrealistic but as e-government became a routine feature of local government, it was no surprise when the target was met. Now it is possible to pay council tax, business rates and parking fines online, as well as download agendas for council meetings, submit planning applications or browse local authority performance data. In the post-2005 target environment, the debate has shifted to *Transformational Local Government* (to give it its 2006 Cabinet Office paper title), which aims to realise engagement with citizens and communities, the reshaping of service delivery and organisational change by July 2007.

7   Children's services

Outline of current duties and status of local education authorities, responsibility for child welfare and development of education system at all tiers.

Education is the biggest service English local government provides, accounting for 34 per cent of all local expenditure in England in 2004/5. It is frequently the most discussed area, thanks to the national emphasis placed upon it by successive governments, and while local councils provide the services, the national framework is subject to constant alteration by the centre in the drive to improve standards. From the Elementary Education Act 1870 to the new trust schools being set up, the way in which local councils provide education has been continually refigured by central government as priorities change on a generational basis. The English state schools system was established under the 1870 Act with the formation of elected school boards to administer free education to children under thirteen, this having previously been undertaken in some areas by the Church. A further Act in 1880 made this compulsory as some parents and employers had obstructed the progress of free education under the threadbare legislation. The Education Act 1902 had the effect of replacing the boards and their chaotic finances with local education authorities (LEAs) at county and county borough level, financed by local taxes. This system remains in place today.

Subsequent reforms increased the age of compulsory education to fourteen in 1929, fifteen in 1947 and sixteen in 1972. In the post-war period, an ideological battle between Labour and Conservative took place over selective versus comprehensive education. The education policies of the Thatcher government in the 1980s were largely based around creating a national policy framework complemented by budgetary independence of schools from LEAs, though some education institutions such as post-sixteen colleges and polytechnics were removed from LEA control. During the first and second terms of the Blair government reforms were largely based around targeted intervention in weak schools and some organisational reform of school status following on from the Conservatives' more radical reforms a decade or so earlier. However, in the third Blair term the government appears to have realised that the educational standards it craves and promised voters will not be delivered by LEAs in their current form, having already removed any budgetary discretion they might have had. Nonetheless, education remains nominally under local government supervision and its biggest service.

The chief education officer is one of the five statutory officers each county and single-tier local authority is required to have by law. Further changes were introduced under the Children's Act 2004 with the creation of director of children's services as a mandatory post. While local authorities remain responsible for education, the chief government department with oversight for education is the Department for Education and Skills (DfES). Following the introduction of direct funding from the DfES, education finance is no longer handled by the Department for Communities and Local Government through grants to local authorities. This section does not deal with England's independent schools, which are not subject to LEA supervision and have differing structures.

Sure Start

Sure Start is a government initiative announced in 1999 in order to 'give children the best start in life'. The programme is a targeted initiative aimed at joining up local social programmes in education and healthcare in the most disadvantaged communities, with Sure Start areas designated according to the index of deprivation. Their activities include childcare, advice and activities for children. The reduction of child poverty is one of the government's key objectives and Sure Start is seen as integral to achieving this goal. In 2006 there were 524 local Sure Start centres and the government has targeted to increase this to 2,500 by 2008 and 3,500 by 2010.

Though Sure Start is overseen jointly by the DfES and the Department for Work and Pensions, there is some indirect local authority involvement at social services level, as well as involvement from other public and voluntary sector partners.

Early years

From April 2004, all children aged three and four have been entitled to local free part-time nursery provision. This is available from public, private or voluntary sector providers on the basis of a minimum 12.5 hours per week for 38 weeks of the year.

Local education authorities

Local education authorities exist among England's 34 county and 116 single-tier local authorities. Under reforms instigated by the Conservative government under the Education Reform Act 1988, some schools opted out of LEA control after parental ballot to become grant-maintained schools (GM schools), directly funded by the Department of Education. Under the School Standards and Framework Act 1998, GM schools were given the choice of becoming foundation schools (funded by the LEA but organisationally independent) or community schools (LEA funded and controlled). The primary role of LEAs is to organise school funding and allocate school places, but these now take place within restrictive national guidelines. They are also responsible for school transport and arranging the education of children with special needs. LEAs are also responsible for funding undergraduate education in the form of assessing tuition fee support and also for funding those studying for postgraduate teacher training.

Until the Education Act 1993, there was a statutory duty to appoint an education committee in each county or metropolitan district council. Though this duty was lifted in the Act, most continued to do so. Under the Local Government Act 2000, education was dealt with by the lead member for education in each council cabinet (county and single tier), replaced since the Children's Act 2004 by the lead member for children's services. Among these authorities most appoint an education or children's services scrutiny committee.

Schools organisation

Education between the ages of four and sixteen is split by age into primary (4–11) and secondary (11–16) levels. The primary level is sometimes sub-divided into infant (4–7) and junior (7–11) schools, and some secondary schools are known as high schools. Some LEAs, mainly rural counties, retain the use of the lower (4 to 8 or 9), middle (8 or 9 to 12 or 13) and upper (12 or 13 to 16) school system. The period of education between the ages of four and sixteen is now banded by years from Reception (age 4–5), then Year 1, the first compulsory year (age 5–6), through to Year 11 (age 15–16). Thus primary schools cover Reception through to Year 6, with secondary education covering Year 7 to Year 11. For the purposes of the National Curriculum tests (also unofficially known as SATs), pupils are banded into key stages, as follows:

- Key Stage 1 (KS1) – during Year 2 (ages 6–7)
- Key Stage 2 (KS2) – towards the end of Year 6 (ages 10–11)
- Key Stage 3 (KS3) – towards the end of Year 9 (ages 13–14)
- Key Stage 4 (KS4) – towards the end of Year 11 (ages 15–16).

The taking of the General Certificate of Secondary Education in different subjects at age sixteen (or possibly fifteen if the child's sixteenth birthday falls after the exam) marks the end of compulsory education. Post-sixteen education at either a sixth form or FE college is neither compulsory nor an LEA responsibility. Prior to entering university at the common entry age of eighteen, students in post-sixteen education generally take the Advanced Level General Certificate of Education (more commonly known as the A-Level), though it is possible to enter higher education at a later age or with a vocational qualification such as a BTEC National Diploma.

Among LEAs in England there are four categories of schools:

- community: conventional LEA-maintained schools with a governing body
- foundation: former GM schools maintained by LEAs but with some independence
- voluntary-aided: religious schools supervised by the LEA but with some independence
- voluntary-controlled: religious schools supervised by the LEA.

There is also one type of secondary school in England not controlled by LEAs: the city academy. These have private sponsors who supervise the running of the school through the governing body they help appoint and are accountable directly to the DfES. A number of city technology colleges, created in the 1980s as a forerunner of the programme, also exist, though these are in the process of being converted into academies. Special schools for those with learning difficulties and disabled children also exist outside the conventional framework but as LEA schools.

Each school, regardless of category, is supervised by a board of school governors, though the composition varies according to type. Governors fall into one of these categories:

- parent governors: parents
- staff governors: members of school staff
- LEA governors: nominated by the LEA
- community governors: members of the local community (appointed by the rest of the governing body)
- foundation and sponsor governors: representatives of any sponsoring bodies.

Local authority education committees were able to co-opt two school governors to sit on them and this system has been retained for education scrutiny committees.

Lifelong learning

Each LEA may also provide adult education on a discretionary basis. These are paid-for (often subsidised) leisure, language or vocational courses at adult education centres. Adults may also enrol at non-LEA further education colleges to pursue such courses and are encouraged to do so as part of the government's lifelong learning programme and targets for increasing the number of university graduates.

Children's trusts

Established under the Children Act 2004, children's trusts are an attempt to bring together all local authority services for children under one single integrated council department, rather than fragmenting them between education and social services, for instance. The impetus for the policy came from the death of eight-year-old Victoria Climbié as a result of poor communications between social services, the health service and the police. The first wave of thirty-five pilot trusts was announced in 2003 and under the 2004 Act all county and single-tier authorities will have a children's trust by 2008. Under the reforms unveiled in the NHS in 2006, most children's trusts will share boundaries with the local NHS primary care trust.

From 2006, each county or single-tier local authority must produce an annual Children and Young People's Plan under the Act, which outlines its strategic corporate approach to children's services, identifies targets for securing better outcomes for young people in that area and is open to inspection by Ofsted. Also from 2006, local safeguarding children boards replace the old area child protection committees as the lead agency for child protection, including children in care, adoption and fostering. Their membership includes local councils, the local NHS and police.

8   Adult care and health

Outline of social care responsibilities and role in public health, including development of provision in these areas.

As well as children's services, county and single-tier authorities also exercise considerable powers over the wellbeing of older people, now organised under the banner of adult care and health. This short chapter will detail the development of this role and the responsibilities currently discharged by authorities at this tier.

Local social services ostensibly began under the Poor Law Act 1601 but in the local government sense they started alongside the creation of the municipal corporations with the Poor Law Amendment Act 1834, which created the boards of guardians, abolished in 1929. County councils acquired the duty to detain and treat the mentally ill in 1890, though this function was transferred to the NHS upon its creation. Local authority social services were formally constituted under the Local Authorities Social Services Act 1970, which made social services departments mandatory.

The lead department for social care issues is the Department for Health.

Social care and health

The National Health Service and Community Care Act 1990 placed local authorities under a new duty to provide social care for the elderly. The term 'social care' defines a plethora of services provided by local authorities and comes in many forms. This can constitute homecare, day centres or residential nursing homes. The term also covers services such as providing meals on wheels to the elderly and home help for people with disabilities. Increasingly, local authorities have transferred social care services into the private sector and the Care Standards Act 2000 laid down the framework for the future of social care, including:

- an independent National Care Standards Commission, to regulate all care homes, private and voluntary healthcare, and a range of social care services in accordance with national minimum standards;
- a General Social Care Council, to raise professional and training standards for the million-strong social care workforce;
- a Training Organisation for Social Services, to improve both the quality and quantity of practice learning opportunities for social work students;
- a Social Care Institute for Excellence, to act as a knowledge base and to promote best practice in social care services.

As well as modernising social care, the trend has also moved towards encouraging supported independent living rather than automatically placing older people in residential care. Recently the introduction of direct payments from local authorities to eligible persons has enabled more choice for older people to decide on how their care package is delivered. Another emphasis is on providing relief for carers of older people by providing home help or adult placement schemes, where the older person is temporarily accommodated elsewhere. There are also many examples of joint working between social services departments and primary care trusts in the NHS in the field of adult care. However, one recent negative development has been 'bed blocking', whereby patients have to remain in hospital longer than necessary following treatment as the local authority cannot find suitable residential care for them. Most local authorities appoint a lead member for adult care and health within the executive and the government has indicated that this role will become mandatory under future legislation as a knock-on effect of the new statutory post of director of adult social services. Local authorities and social care providers are inspected by the Commission for Social Care Inspection.

Better Government for Older People

The Better Government for Older People initiative is an ongoing programme to better integrate the needs of older people in an ageing society into the work of government at all levels. Launched by the Cabinet Office in 1998, its work is continued by the Better Government for Older People Partnership and its Older People's Advisory Group, elected from local older people's forums across England, and it works across central and local government and the voluntary sector to promote independent living and citizenship through social inclusion.

9   Regeneration and infrastructure

Outline of powers and duties in relation to sustainable communities, housing, planning and development control, environmental protection, passenger transport authorities and roads.

Local government has come a long way since the legislation passed in 1855 to set up London's Metropolitan Board of Works and that of 1868 to allow councils to demolish unsanitary housing, with England's town planning system often marvelled at by other countries. The social reforms of the public health movement in the Victorian age led to local government playing a key role in environmental health in England's rapidly growing urban centres. Town planning was also formalised as a discipline through the pioneering work of Ebenezer Howard, the architect of the garden cities, whose influence on urbanism is still felt today. From the time of the creation of the municipal corporations in 1835, local government was given increased powers over housing on an almost generational basis in 1868, 1890, 1909, 1919 and 1936, while the town planning aspect first introduced in 1909 was improved in 1919, 1925 and 1932, with the current familiar system of planning permission created in the landmark Act of 1947. Following the

Second World War, the new towns were conceived to address housing shortages and stimulate regional economies, being built around London in the late 1940s and elsewhere in the early 1960s. In 1968 passenger transport authorities were created in large urban centres in England (what would become the metropolitan counties) and in 1980 urban development corporations were set up in eight economically depressed areas. Until recently, the Office of the Deputy Prime Minister, the department of state responsible for local government, had a distinctly urban focus under the banner of 'creating sustainable communities' (of which more later). Since 1997, in fact, the number of initiatives and policies are too numerous to list here and are best dealt with in the sections below.

Sustainable communities

The current government's policies around urban issues, particularly regeneration and infrastructure, are guided by its definition of 'sustainable communities'. The blueprint for this set of policies is the Communities Plan, published as *Sustainable Communities: Building for the Future* (Office of the Deputy Prime Minister, 2003), and it defines a sustainable community as one in which there are:

- decent homes at prices people can afford;
- good public transport;
- schools, hospitals and shops;
- a clean, safe environment.

The plan earmarked four growth areas, in the south-east of England, to be used for a massive programme of new house building to tackle regional shortages. The four growth areas are Ashford in Kent (which already houses the Ashford International rail station for

Eurostar services), the London-Stansted-Cambridge-Peterborough corridor along the M11 and A1, Milton Keynes and the south Midlands, and the Thames Gateway. The Thames Gateway also contains the 2012 Olympic Park at Stratford. The plan also specifies a programme of housing market renewal, whereby regions with low housing demand in the north and the Midlands will see targeted demolition of vacant properties.

Housing

Local authority housing management is dealt with at district and single-tier level and it continues to be a key responsibility among these tiers, though the concept of municipal ownership of housing has largely given way to the idea of social housing among a diverse sector. The introduction by the Conservatives of the council tenant's right to buy during the 1980s formed the first attack on the concept and local authority housing stock has dwindled ever since, though Labour has altered the landscape through its emphasis on the social housing sector rather than returning to wholesale municipal owner-ship. Local councils still retain a considerable and ageing housing stock, however, and recent government policy was in favour of externalising the burden of improvement to a decent standard to either other social partners (by tenants opting out to housing associations) or the private sector (in the form of private finance initiatives). Another model was the arm's-length management organisation (ALMO), whereby new agencies were set up to manage homes on behalf of the authority but with the authority retaining ownership. Progress towards achieving the creation of new ALMOs proved slow on account of councillor and tenant resistance and, faced with the 2010 target for all council homes to be of a decent standard, the government caved in and accepted that councils should be able to finance improvements another way.

On a regional level, regional housing boards are responsible for preparing regional housing strategies and advising ministers on allocations of funds to finance housing capital improvements from the regional housing pot. These boards consist of representatives of the regional assembly, government agencies and the Housing Corporation, a non-departmental public body under the supervision of the Department for Communities and Local Government. In 2005 the Treasury-commissioned Review of Housing Supply, led by Kate Barker, reported and proposed that the regional housing boards be merged with regional planning boards. The government also proposed, in response to the review that new builds increase from 150,000 to 200,000 per year, that developers be charged a planning gain supplement in order to fund necessary new infrastructure. Social housing provision in the rented sector (housing associations) is regulated by the Housing Corporation.

Planning and development control

Britain's pioneering town planning system, particularly the green belt, was once the envy of the world and has evolved steadily since the Second World War. The Town and Country Planning Act 1947 introduced the elementary principles of council-framed plans and also introduced the duty on local authorities to manage development in their locality through planning consent, ending the automatic right to develop one's own land. The Act also introduced the listed building system, whereby buildings of special significance are protected from modification or demolition. The Town and Country Planning Act 1990 consolidated changes since the introduction of the regime, most notably the Section 106 arrangements to allow councils to compel developers to make infrastructure improvements around new building, including the construction of community facilities, where the knock-on effect of such development can be proven (the so-called 'planning gain'). The planning gain system is currently under review and a planning gain levy on new development is also strongly mooted. District and single-tier authorities are responsible for forming quasi-judicial planning committees and sub-committees (in the case of smaller applications) to hear and decide on local planning issues.

The Planning and Compulsory Purchase Act 2004, the first ever to be carried over from one session of parliament to another, introduced sweeping changes to the planning system, largely around strategic plans (modelled to some extent on the London Plan introduced under the Greater London Authority Act). Under the former planning regime, each local authority had to prepare a local plan – the development plan in the case of districts, structure plans in the case of counties and unitary development plans (a hybrid of development and structure plans) in the case of single-tier authorities. The new system entails the production of a local development framework (LDF) by each planning authority (district, single tier and national parks) which sets out the authority's policies on development and land use within the locality. Under the reforms, which were intended to coincide with the move towards elected regional government in England, county councils lost their main role in the planning process in that county structure plans were abolished in favour of regional spatial strategies (RSSs), though they still retain powers over mineral and waste planning. The RSS is instead formulated by the regional planning body (RPB), which is one of the eight indirectly elected regional assemblies sitting for that purpose. Counties also retain a role in making representations to RPBs over issues affecting their jurisdiction. LDFs must be carried out in with regard to the RSS.

Environmental protection

Waste collection is undertaken by district and single-tier authorities but then managed and disposed of by either the county tier (in the case of districts) or joint arrangements through waste authorities (single tier). The provision of cemeteries and crematoriums is handled by districts and single-tier authorities, as are clean air monitoring and environmental protection issues, including the enforcement of fly-tipping and industrial pollution (though with regard to the Environment Agency and the Health and Safety Executive's roles in large incidents).

Local transport

In 1968 passenger transport authorities (PTAs) were set up in six English metropolitan areas (what would become the metropolitan counties six years later) under the Transport Act of that year to take over local authority bus services and local rail networks. Six years later the PTAs were abolished and their functions transferred to the metropolitan county councils but on their abolition in 1986 the bodies were reintroduced. The PTA acts as the council-appointed accountable element to the services provided by the passenger transport executives (PTEs) in each of these areas. One PTE directly provides transport services in the form of the Tyne and Wear Metro railway while the Merseyside PTE operates the ferry service. Others do not operate local public transport but instead provide information services such as timetables and travel centres.

The Transport Act 1985 was introduced to liberalise the local bus market and this had the effect of effectively ending the council provision of bus services in all but a handful of local authorities. Similarly, most council-run airports were forced into the hands of consortiums under the liberalisation agenda, though some local authority airport groups (most notably Manchester, which is owned by all the councils in Greater Manchester) have emerged as key players in this market in their own right.

Highways

County and single-tier councils are responsible for the maintenance of all local roads (major and minor) falling under their jurisdiction, as well as traffic management, parking and road safety. Trunk roads are the responsibility of central government through the Highways Agency of the Department for Transport.

10   Community and culture

Outline of powers in relation to culture, sport and licensing.
Also duties around community safety and community cohesion.
Consumer protection and environmental health. Voluntary
sector.

Local authorities are in a unique position to influence the shaping of their communities, in terms not only of the built environment but also of its social fabric. Though local councils are primarily engaged in education, social services and environmental functions, a number of activities also take place under what could be termed 'community services'.

Leisure, culture and sport

The most common leisure function associated with local government is libraries, which are provided at county and single-tier level. The building of public libraries by councils was first permitted in 1850, though not the stocking of them (which was only laid down in law in 1919), and as such most of England's libraries during that era were built by philanthropic benefactors. Today the emphasis has shifted from merely lending books to lifelong learning and

tensions. Although ostensibly replacing the defunct term 'race relations' (which had already become questioned by practitioners before 9/11), several definitions exist, of which this is the most succinct: 'A cohesive community is a community that is in a state of wellbeing, harmony and stability. Local authorities have an important role in facilitating community cohesion, through listening to communities, engaging residents and assisting interaction between communities' (Improvement and Development Agency glossary).

An array of funds and initiatives exist to assist local authorities at all levels to undertake this work and the new Department for Communities and Local Government places great emphasis on it and the need for local authority leadership in this area.

Consumer protection

The Sunday Trading Act 1994 requires county and single-tier councils to enforce the opening hours of large shops (above 280 square metres trading area) on Sundays to ensure they open only between 10 a.m. and 6 p.m. for no longer than six hours. District and single-tier authorities are charged with the licensing of local markets. The county and single-tier level discharge the consumer protection function of local authorities, such as food labelling, fair trading, weights and measures, trades descriptions and consumer advice. The Department for Trade and Industry is the lead central government department on these issues.

Environmental health

Local government takes its environmental health role seriously. District and single-tier authorities are responsible for the inspection of retail establishments under their duty to ensure food safety, with the power to issue enforcement notices to demand either improvement or cessation of activities in cases where inspections demonstrate negligence to ensure food hygiene. They are also responsible for dealing with dangerous dogs and vermin and insect infestations, as well as animal health concerning the movement of livestock.

Voluntary sector

Local councils have long given grants to community groups to provide complimentary services to the community such as social services (day centres), consumer advice (Citizens Advice Bureaux) or arts provision (concert halls), often in exchange for local authority representation on their boards. The relationship between local councils and the local voluntary sector was formalised with the introduction of local compacts. Compacts exist in most councils, though the extent of the arrangement and its partners tend to vary.

Registration

The administration of registration districts in order to register births, deaths, marriages and civil partnerships is the responsibility of either county or single-tier authorities under the national direction of the General Register Office. Since 2004 they have also been responsible for organising citizenship ceremonies on behalf of newly naturalised British citizens.

11 Regional and neighbourhood governance

Role of Greater London Authority, regional assemblies and regional development agencies (including economic development), city regions agenda, community governance (also town and parish councils), New Deal for Communities and the concept of 'governance'.

This chapter will deal with the emergence of supplemental tiers of sub-national and sub-principal governance which enhance the work of local government. Though these are relatively new, introduced for the most part since 1997, some have their antecedents in previous policies, proposals and structures. All have been touted as detrimental to the existence of local government in its current form, though local government has for the most part engaged with them when required to do so by national government. Principally, the introduction of English regional government, begun modestly as an intended self-contained reform with the government office network by the Conservatives in 1994, has been driven in part as a response to the 'English question' and also as a means to promote regional economic growth after several decades of zero co-ordination of regional economic policy by the centre, with resulting social consequences. Similarly, the emergence of community governance has been driven both by the demand for increased participation in local affairs and the emphasis on local action to tackle anti-social behaviour and promote liveability.

The Greater London Authority

As the successor to the London County Council (1889–1965), the Greater London Council (GLC, 1965–86) was conceived as a strategic tier of local government covering the all-purpose London boroughs, with some ad hoc joint arrangements in housing and education. Following the abolition of the GLC in 1986, its powers were dispersed between the boroughs (housing, and education in inner London – outer London boroughs had always been responsible for their own education facilities), central government (transport) and some joint arrangements (planning and waste). The resumption of this strategic tier in 2000, following the 1998 referendum which paved its creation, saw the old GLC boundaries observed by the new Greater London Authority (GLA), which did not resemble its predecessor in terms of providing direct services, though the GLC similarly did not enjoy the indirect supervisory powers over the Metropolitan Police and London Fire Brigade that the GLA now does.

While the GLC sat as a conventional county-style council of ninety-two seats, headed by a leader and overseen by committees, the governance model of the GLA is split between the office of the directly elected mayor of London and the 25-member London Assembly, which performs scrutiny of the mayor and provides some members of the functional bodies of the 'GLA family' (see below). The mayor of London is directly elected for four-year terms by voters across Greater London; the current mayor, Ken Livingstone, was elected an as independent in 2000 and again in 2004, this time as the Labour candidate (the Conservatives' Steve Norris came second on both occasions). The system of election used is the supplementary vote, where each voter expresses a first and second preference and if no candidate has 50 per cent or more first preferences then the second preferences of all candidates are reallocated to the two highest ranked candidates to determine the winner. The primary role of the mayor is to draft the statutory strategies of the GLA (including the overarching London Plan) and to set the budget for the core GLA and the functional bodies (the Metropolitan Police Authority, the London Fire and Emergency Planning Authority, Transport for London and the London Development Agency), as well as appointing members to these bodies. The mayor also appoints a deputy from among the members of the London Assembly. The mayor of London should not be confused with the ancient office of the Lord Mayor of the City of London Corporation.

The London Assembly is elected alongside the mayor, also for a four-year term, under the additional member system. Fourteen members represent geographical constituencies based on groupings of London boroughs while the remaining eleven are elected from a London-wide list. Parties may replace members from the list in the event of a resignation while the constituency section requires a by-election should this occur. The results of the 2004 election and the current representation are shown in Table 11.1.

The assembly has the power to veto the mayor's budget if two-thirds of members vote to do so. It also has input into the mayor's strategies and supplies members for the mayor to appoint to the functional bodies. Its other main role is to scrutinise the activities of the GLA and other public service providers (such as the NHS but also companies such as Thames Water plc) in Greater London through the works of its committees and panels. The assembly has the sole right to appoint the staff of the core GLA, aside from a handful of political appointments by the mayor.

Table 11.1: Party representation in London Assembly, 2006

Party	Constituency seats	London-wide list seats	Total
Conservative	9	0	9
Labour	5	2	7
Liberal Democrat	5	0	5
Green	0	2	2
One London*	0	2	2

* elected 2004 as UK Independence Party

The London Fire and Emergency Planning Authority was also introduced as a functional body under the GLA Act and replaced the London Fire and Civil Defence Authority as the capital's fire and rescue authority. It consists of seventeen members, nine from the London Assembly and eight from the boroughs. The Metropolitan Police Authority (MPA) was also created in 2000 to take over the Home Secretary's unique role of a one-person police authority. Its twenty-three members are appointed by the mayor from the London Assembly (twelve), the Greater London Magistrates Association from the capital's justices of the peace (four) and the Home Secretary (one independent member); a further six independent members are recruited openly by public appointment. The MPA provides accountability and sets the budget and strategy of the Metropolitan Police but the Metropolitan Police Service, whose commissioner remains appointed by the Home Secretary, remains operationally independent. The London Development Agency (LDA) is led by a board of fourteen members, all appointed by the mayor. Its role is the formulation and realisation of the mayor's economic development strategy. Finally, in 2000 Transport for London (TfL) assumed the role previously undertaken by London Transport, though London Underground was not passed to its control until 2003, because of complexities surrounding the PPP maintenance deal and Livingstone's opposition to this. TfL now also supervises the Public Carriage Office for the licensing of taxis in the capital, which was previously part of the Metropolitan Police.

Bodies such as the Port of London Authority are independent of the Greater London Authority. The Government Office for London remains in place post-GLA and continues to play a liaison and co-ordination role between central government, the GLA and the London boroughs. Following a commitment in its May 2005 election manifesto, the government announced a review of the GLA's powers in November of that year, which completed its consultation in February 2006, having received submissions from the GLA (both mayor and assembly) and the Association of London Government.

In 2006, the government published its conclusion of a year-long review of the GLA's powers, as promised in the 2005 election manifesto. In particular, it is proposed that the mayor will now have powers to intervene in the planning policies of the thirty-three local councils in the capital and arbitrate on planning decisions of strategic importance. Social housing in London, currently supervised by the London Housing Board, will pass to the mayor, who will also oversee spending on housing investment and creating more affordable housing. A new London Skills and Employment Board, chaired by the mayor, will enable him to fulfil his new statutory duty to promote the skills base in the capital. The new London Waste and Recycling Forum will see the mayor, the boroughs and the capital's waste authorities sit together to monitor performance and ensure compliance with the mayor's waste strategy.

Regional governance

The Greater London Authority is ostensibly England's first and, thus far, only elected regional government. The process by which it was created before going live in 2000, such as the 1997 White Paper and the 1998 referendum on its introduction, was subsequently attempted outside of the capital.

Outside London, which has its own regional development agency (RDA) in the form of the LDA, there are eight RDAs, which promote, *inter alia*, economic regeneration and investment at the regional level. Created following a 1998 White Paper and the Regional Development Agencies Act 1998, these are each held to account and scrutinised by a regional assembly (previously regional chamber) which consists of 70 per cent nominated local councillors from across each region and 30 per cent special interest groups from the business, education and voluntary sectors. Each regional assembly also performs the functions required of regional planning bodies in the production of the statutory regional spatial strategy under the Planning and Compulsory Purchase Act 2004. Members of the regional assemblies also sit on regional housing boards alongside representatives of the Housing Corporation and government agencies, with responsibility for preparing regional housing strategies and advising ministers on allocations of funds to finance housing capital improvements from the regional housing pot.

In 2002 the government issued a White Paper on introducing elected regional assemblies to regions of England outside London with powers over sustainable development, economic development, spatial planning, transport, waste, housing, culture (including tourism) and biodiversity. The Regional Assemblies Preparations Act 2003 then laid the basis for the staging of referendums in each region, subject to work being undertaken by the Boundary

Committee on the required reform of local government along unitary lines of any region assenting to the introduction of an elected assembly. The government proposed an initial wave of referendums in northern England, where it assumed the highest levels of regional identity and support for elected assemblies, beginning with the North East in November 2004 and followed by the North West and Yorkshire & the Humber, having previously proposed to hold them all on the same day. Following the production of two sets of proposals for future unitary local government in the three regions and the establishment of official 'yes' and 'no' campaigns granted equal funding by the Electoral Commission, the two-question referendum was held in the North East by all-postal ballot on 4 November 2004. Having rejected the proposal by almost four to one (696,519 votes to 197,310), the government then announced that the other two scheduled referendums would not take place before the statutory time limit (under the 2003 Act) of June 2005, effectively ending the policy. The government has since stated it has no intention of seeking their introduction.

The regional boundaries of England were set in 1994 under the creation of the government office network, established to promote better working of departments of state at regional level. The network remains in place some twelve years on and a recent review affirmed the government's intentions to retain it, albeit with some stream-lining. The network plays a significant role in relation to local authorities and communications from government departments. Furthermore, fire control services have been reorganised into regional units based on these regions, while the Home Office has attempted to reorganise police forces along largely regional lines. In 2006 the government reorganised the NHS's sub-national activities into region-based strategic health authorities and ambulance trusts, with the further addition of the new post of regional director of public health. European parliamentary representation in England is based on the nine recognised regions also, using the closed regional list system to elect England's allocation of MEPs.

City regions

As a response to the failure to promote the take-up of elected regional assemblies in England, the intellectual current within the governing New Labour party and its associated think tanks around local democracy issues (such as the New Local Government Network and the Centre for Cities) began to come to the view that 'city regions' might be the best means by which to secure better regional co-ordination and revitalise local government. Though the term 'city region' has been in use among economists, planners and urbanists throughout the post-war period, in a UK context the term arrived with Derek Senior's lengthy *Memorandum of Dissent* against the Redcliffe-Maud report in 1969, with Senior proposing a city regional framework instead of Redcliffe-Maud's proposals for a unitary system of local government and eight provincial councils. In the 1974 reorganisation of local government by the Conservative government of Edward Heath, which dismissed the Redcliffe-Maud report of its predecessor, the resulting two-tier system saw a partial city regional system emerge under the metropolitan counties, which were later abolished alongside the GLC by Margaret Thatcher in 1986. Today, the vestiges of the late-1960s appetite for city regions remain in the passenger transport authorities in the former metropolitan counties. Currently, the Department for Communities and Local Government (DCLG) has factored city regions into its workplan through its Core Cities Group and the Northern Way regeneration initiative across the three northern RDAs.

It is said that the forthcoming and delayed 2006 local government

White Paper will very much have a city regional flavour and ministerial speeches have trailed its contents to that effect, the government having already hinted at this direction in the *State of the English Cities* report earlier in the year. The emphasis of the government's agenda is very much around allowing city regions to emerge from below in an asymmetrical fashion, such as grafting alternative arrangements on different conurbations to reflect local circumstance – a Black Country 'senate' of West Midlands local councils might wish to pursue a different road to Newcastle–Gateshead, for instance. However, the question of leadership is always at the forefront of such debates, with the idea of each city region being led by an elected mayor or a similar arrangement proving popular with the government, not least because of the record of the GLA in securing effective change. Competitiveness against European rivals is of interest here; this is already driving much of the DCLG's urban agenda, with government studies looking at how city regions work elsewhere in Europe, such as the Association of the Urban Region of Stuttgart and the Lille agglomeration.

As with any form of local government reorganisation, city regions have their discontents, mostly local councillors in the cities concerned, but also in opposition parties and even the Treasury, who are said to oppose the devolution of powers and resources required.

Local strategic partnerships

It was a condition for the eighty-eight areas receiving Neighbourhood Renewal funding that to receive additional funding they had to establish a multi-agency local strategic partnership (LSP). Each LSP was constituted of representatives from the following sectors:

- public sector organisations (the local authority, the local police and fire brigade, Jobcentre Plus, the local primary care trust);
- private companies (particularly if they are major employers);
- business organisations;
- the community and voluntary sector.

From the mandatory eighty-eight first introduced, their number increased to over 360 by the time of the Office of the Deputy Prime Minister's five-year appraisal of their existence. The impetus for the creation of LSPs was to facilitate better joined-up working at the local level and to bring about the desired culture change for local councils to realise their role as one of several agencies working at this level. The emphasis for the next stage of their development is very much concerned with aligning their work and role with that of local area agreements, so that each partnership could become the primary voice for the local public sector in their area and play a delivery co-ordination role. The government would also like to see their work geared towards the sustainable communities agenda in the longer term, rather than just administering lapsed regeneration initiatives as Neighbourhood Renewal runs its course.

Community governance

In some councils where no parish tier exists, there has been some experimentation with representative local area forums, which often go under specific local names or are termed 'community councils'. As there is no statutory requirement for this, their powers, basis (community or councillor led) and resourcing can vary across England, from expansive to threadbare, not least because of budgetary pressures. The Clean Neighbourhoods and Environment

Act 2005 also increased the powers of parish and town councils to deal with anti-social behaviour.

Again, as part of the delayed 2006 White Paper, the government has indicated its preference for the next stage of new localism in the form of 'double devolution' (i.e. devolution from Whitehall to local councils and then to the community level). This was already floated in the 2005 ODPM 'local:vision' reports, which called for communities to be able to trigger action in unresponsive local public services and to enable greater ownership of assets by local communities. Though couched in the rhetoric of empowerment, at this stage there is little policy detail or concrete proposals to report on but the concept of sub-principal delivery units promises to be a key motif for the next stage of New Labour's local government agenda, with the possibility of all England being covered by community councils, not just parished areas.

New Deal for Communities

As with the Sure Start programme, the New Deal for Communities is targeted at areas that score highest on the multiple deprivation index. Since the programme was first announced in 1998, £2 billion has been invested into it. As opposed to immediately tangible physical regeneration, its emphasis is on social capital and increasing capacity within the community. Guided by the National Strategy for Neighbourhood Renewal, each of the thirty-nine New Deal for Communities partnerships exists across one or more wards within a local authority. Alongside the representatives of the local authority on the partnership there is a non-partisan elected element to allow for community involvement in their running. These are the newest form for local democracy, alongside the elected foundation hospital trusts.

Mapping 'governance'

Unlike in the past, we cannot now simply speak of 'local government' but must instead acknowledge that local councils are but one of several agencies operating at the local level in the public services. This brings us on to the concept of 'local governance'. As central governments of all persuasions have reformed the public sector over the past twenty-five years, scant regard has been given to the need for elected accountability when compared to perceived effectiveness of being fit for purpose. Instead, in what has been dubbed the explosion of the 'quango state', the proliferation of local units of administration has been driven entirely by the whims of the centre and often without any reference to existing roles of local government, instead placing them in the hands of centrally accountable units. Table 11.2 gives a partial overview based on current tiers of local government as to how this process has taken place and how each unit is represented within its organisation and interacts with others.

Table 11.2: Governance of local public services in 2006

	Local	County	Regional
Representatives	District or unitary	County	Regional assembly or Greater London Authority
Children's services	Children's trust; Sure Start; local safeguarding children board	Children's trust; local safeguarding children board	
Education	Further and higher education corporations; non-LEA schools	Learning and Skills Council, Connexions Partnership	
Emergency services	Borough command unit; Crime and Disorder Reduction Partnership	Police and fire authorities	Fire control
Health	Primary care trust	Primary care trust	Strategic health authority; ambulance trust
Housing	Arm's-length management organisations; registered social landlords		Regional housing board
Multi-agency working	Local strategic partnership	Local strategic partnership	Government office
Planning	Local development framework		Regional planning body
Regeneration	Business improvement district; New Deal for Communities; urban development corporation		Regional development agency
Transport		Passenger transport authority	

12   Policy context

Examination of party policies and attitudes towards local government, recent developments and signposts for reform.

Writing about British local government has been said to be akin to aiming at a constantly moving target. As we have seen, under Britain's unwritten constitution local government can be (and is) subject to constant reform directed from the centre. Even so, there are a number of constants and embedded policy trends that can be discerned from each political party. This chapter considers the recent history of change and how parties have reacted to it.

Policy direction over local government (except in the case of the Liberal Democrats, for obvious reasons) tends to reflect a party's national standing in relation to its results at general elections rather than local polls. However, a number of other factors can creep in, for instance the Major government's backtracking on the introduction of unitary councils in shire areas following backbench pressure from MPs representing rural constituencies, or activist unease over elected mayors in the Labour Party leading to lukewarm support among Labour parliamentarians, rendering such policies unpopular outside Downing Street. Of course, it is possible to trace policies that have made it to the statute books despite lacking wider support, Margaret Thatcher's community charge/poll tax being the obvious case in point.

For the early post-war period certainly, local government as a political institution existed in a policy vacuum as a key agency of the social democratic consensus, with reform deferred until the early 1970s and only minor differences in policy over questions of structure, mainly around tiers rather than powers. While Thatcher's Conservative government embarked upon an immediate collision course with local government, introducing rate capping, urban development corporations and the grandstanding *Streamlining the Cities* White Paper of 1983, it was Labour (in the form of Anthony Crosland) who ushered in the era of fiscal restraint, by which local government was expected to dance to central government's tune, which has remained in place to this day, regardless of government. In any case, it is possible to argue that local government's sphere of influence is receding to the point whereby the debate is concerned with an ever-decreasing number of direct service issues and questions of management, rather than anything on the ideological scale of Section 28 or the poll tax.

Given local government's status as a side-issue in terms of national political debate and its esoteric interest to wonks rather than voters, it is often more worthwhile observing the debate that takes place around the parties in policy networks and think tanks and where necessary this chapter will reference that. During the 1980s, for instance, the Local Government Information Unit emerged as a Labour council-funded campaigning think tank in response to the raft of Thatcherite policies perceived as an assault on local democracy, advocating policies in step with Labour generally at that time. During the 1990s, it was supplanted by the thinking emerging from the New Local Government Network, a think tank funded in part by private sector contractors advocating distinctly Blairite policies around modernisation and private finance, which played a key role in getting the much-vaunted 'new localism' on the agenda.

The revival in the fortunes of the Conservative Party at the national level under David Cameron's leadership, following steady progress in local polls, has seen the Policy Exchange think tank advancing a Tory variant of localism (in contrast to the general lack of ideas in the wider party), such as resisting regionalised policing, though this 'localism' has also manifested itself in areas such as the right of councils to reintroduce the measures laid out in Section 28. Within the Liberal Democrats, the CentreForum group has facilitated debate around localism as the party continues its own modernisation. Like local government itself, the think tanks and their standing within policy debates are subject to constant evolution.

Recent developments

New Labour entered power in 1997 with a clear commitment to accept the spending limits set down by the Conservatives and a less clear picture of to what extent they would accept the local government reforms undertaken by the Tories and the culture these left in their wake. In office, however, New Labour acted in the spirit of the ethos contained in New Public Management, as evidenced by the introduction of the Best Value regime and the aplomb by which it pursued target setting to an extent not seen under the Tories. The Conservatives, for their part, slowly appeared to jettison their virtual antipathy to local democracy as their share of councillors increased and as ministerial office became an ever more distant memory. However, as New Labour introduced a raft of reforms which were resisted at every turn by the Tories to the extent that their limited parliamentary votes would permit, what was seen was a distinct lack of ideas. At the time, the commitments to scrap Best Value and comprehensive performance assessment (CPA) appeared as nothing short of a scorched earth policy on the part of the Conservatives.

More recently they have managed to articulate their view that such measures represent a straitjacket by which non-Tory councils can be cajoled into accepting the traditional Tory yardsticks of value for money and efficiency in local public services, something which in their view is best left for the ballot box. While some Tories have shifted in their view of devolution and now support the London Assembly (albeit with the policy of electing it by first past the post rather than proportional representation), others, particularly in London local government, would like to see it replaced by an assembly or 'senate' of borough leaders.

The Liberal Democrats appeared to share the Conservatives' disdain for external inspection and target setting, proposing instead a lighter-touch regime of self-assessment and peer review overseen by an independent but strengthened Audit Commission. Similarly, they and the Tories have resisted the trend towards having more elected mayors as a means to achieve stronger city leadership, though David Cameron did set out his stall as a mayoral enthusiast during his leadership bid and has since promoted their virtues. This trend among the modernisers within the Tory party, evidenced by their support for elected sheriffs, has come from the localist thinking of bodies such as the Policy Exchange, which has proven to been influential under both Cameron's and Michael Howard's leaderships. However, its overarching proposals for a 'big bang' of wholesale decentralisation from Whitehall, authored by mayoral enthusiast Simon Jenkins, look unlikely to find favour under any administration, in spite of their democratic credentials and possible desirability. As Labour have slowly picked up the pace on promoting elected mayors, not least in the light of experience in the five or so years since the first set were elected, it would seem that opposition to mayoral governance is not as entrenched as previously, though the think tank bubble inhabited by both parties is not necessarily connected to the activist base and the proof will be in the enactment of future legislation.

Furthermore, under Cameron's leadership the Tories have started to appreciate the fact that the current local government setup is overwhelmingly dependent on Westminster and Whitehall for the tools to get things such as new light rail schemes off the ground. It may be purely coincidental, as they are in opposition, but currently the Conservatives are of a more localist bent than Labour in these areas, the Department for Transport happily seeing city regeneration squandered through its refusal to finance new light rail projects in northern cities. As with education reform, however, there appears to be some consensus between Labour and the Tories on the diminishing role of local councils as local education authorities, the weakening of recent reforms in that direction undertaken only at the behest of Labour backbenchers.

Considering that its usual terrain of elected mayors and associated modernisation is positively old hat, the (not so) New Local Government Network has been considering other reforms of late, such as including local councillors in a reformed House of Lords. Issues such as e-government appear to have run their course as a 'sexy' policy area, being an accepted and much-vaunted dimension of customer interface between local authorities and service users and having achieved the target set for 2005 on e-enabled services. On this issue there appears to be no party divide or discussion, save for agreement that it is a 'good thing'. The same could be said for most external calls to open up the local political process and allow for more citizen participation; this tends to be an area where the Liberal Democrats have traditionally been more active, though New Labour has been known to favour innovation through citizens' juries and the like. Again, this has been regarded as the realm of think tank deliberation rather than the result of any groundswell among local councillors or activists. With e-government already largely yesterday's news, predictions of increased citizen participation in local affairs via ICT have not been matched by any sufficient evidence subsequently and, like its sibling the citizens' jury/local referendum, it has slid almost out of view.

In particular, there has been outright hostility from representatives of all three main parties towards the 'double devolution' (from Whitehall to town hall and then to community level) proposals emanating from the then Office of the Deputy Prime Minister during David Miliband's brief tenure as *de facto* secretary of state. Though this latest manifestation of localism has been advocated by a number of bodies for over a decade, its adoption by central government saw councillors shriek in horror at the idea of handing down powers to 'unaccountable' community bodies.

On the question of accountability itself, a key watchword of New Labour's reform efforts, Blair himself was convinced of the need to move councils into an annual election cycle (whereby one councillor per ward is up for re-election every year) but has moved away in the opposite direction since, concurring in its 'local:vision' documents with the Electoral Commission's recommendation of all-out elections every four years across England. Needless to say this has not proven popular with some councillors or opposition parties (though any discussion of reforming elections usually leads to accusations of 'gerrymandering' by a wronged party somewhere along the line). The Standards Board and its accompanying regime have also received non-stop criticism for their work since the board's inception in 2001, hardly surprising as this may be. Its future does appear to be safe under Labour, however, despite a brief period of a ministerial axe looming over it under the weight of constant criticism.

Housing is one field where the contrasts between Labour and the

Conservatives have gradually diminished, Labour appearing to go beyond the Tory reforms of the 1980s in their insistence that local authorities externalise the running of their housing stock and become strategic rather than commissioning authorities, with only the Liberal Democrats left to defend municipal ownership. Of late, with backbench Labour MPs and activists demanding the abandonment of this controversial policy, New Labour has weakened its resolve on externalising as much housing stock as possible by 2010 and a future Labour administration may see this abandoned altogether.

Of course, the *sine qua non* of dividing lines between the parties is the question of restructuring, the unfinished business bequeathed to Labour by the Tories in 1997 following the disastrous Banham Review only a few years earlier. When elected regional government remained on the agenda, John Prescott argued that 'regionalism means reorganisation', yet it has since seemed that reorganisation means regionalism. While the government's regional government proposals were soundly defeated in the North East referendum of October 2004, regionalism has continued apace in the form of fire control mergers and the mergers of strategic health authorities and ambulance trusts along regional lines, coupled with the strengthening of regional offices under the recent review. The November 2004 referendum result took the Liberal Democrats and their decade-old regional government plans by surprise to the point that they still haven't been able to formulate an alternative policy as an answer to the 'English question', though they remain committed to democratising the regions by addressing the democratic deficit in governance by quango. The Conservatives remain implacably opposed to regional government in all its forms (beyond the regional office network they created) and prefer debates around English votes for English laws when asked the 'English question'. In theory, at the last general election, the official position of all three parties was that none would reorganise English local government where two-tier structures remain, though Labour's policy in this area was deliberately somewhat vague. Since then, however, while the Conservatives and Liberal Democrats remain opposed to reorganisation along unitary lines, the government has floated the idea of voluntary mergers in the remaining two-tier areas in order to finally solve the issue of England's variable patchwork of local authorities. This has been presented as a 'generational opportunity' predicated on the need for 'coterminosity' and efficiency in the public services.

The 2005 election manifestos

In its 2005 general election manifesto (*Britain: Forward not Back*), the Labour Party mapped out the thinking on local government for the third term it eventually secured. The document committed Labour to retaining Best Value and CPA while reducing the number of inspectorates. On the question of local government finance, it stated the party's commitment to observing the outcome of the Lyons Review by offering a vague commitment to reforming council tax but ultimately not offering any form of radical replacement such as a local income tax. It also confirmed the party's belief in restraint by promising to continue capping, but only in order to 'protect council taxpayers' while promising to increase central government spending to local councils by introducing three-yearly grants. In terms of sub-national governance, the manifesto was more explicit, stating the abandonment of the goal of introducing elected regional assemblies but promising to retain and reform the powers of existing unelected regional bodies. The party also offered to consult on the question of city regional structures, affirming its belief that mayoral governance leads to stronger leadership. A more specific commitment came in the form of promising to review the powers and role of the Greater London Authority in the light of experience. Labour also set out their stall on neighbourhood governance, promising neighbourhood improvement districts and more powers for communities over local affairs. On the question of local elections, the manifesto confirmed the move towards a unified four-yearly elections cycle.

Continuing their avowed scorched earth policy towards many of New Labour's reforms, the Conservatives' manifesto (*Time for Action*) indicated that the party would abolish both Best Value and CPA, relying instead on the work of inspectorates and accountability via the ballot box. Having introduced the council tax, the party stated its belief in retaining the tax but said that it would abolish capping. The manifesto also promised to abolish all regional structures outside London introduced since 1998 and pass their powers to county councils. It also promised to abolish the Standards Board for England, a longstanding Tory gripe, and pass more powers to local councils from Whitehall, particularly over gypsy and traveller encampments. In terms of local consumer choice, the party sought to reassume its mantle of the right to buy by offering to extend the scheme to housing association tenants. Finally, the policy on 'elected sheriffs' gained an outing in the manifesto as part of a promise to increase local accountability.

The Liberal Democrats' election prospectus (*The* Real *Alternative*) was heavy on promises to liberate local councils from stifling central control, starting with reducing the burden of inspection by merging all inspectorates in an independent Audit Commission. Consistent with the party's longstanding policy to abolish the council tax and replace it with a local income tax, the manifesto promised to transfer local taxation into the Inland Revenue, as well as replacing business rates with a new local site value rate. Capping would also be abolished. The party also promised to transfer powers from unelected quangos to local councils (as well as the healthcare-planning role of primary care trusts), while remaining regional functions would receive local democratic oversight. It would also reform local governance by moving English and Welsh council elections to the single transferable vote system (as for Scotland from 2007) and allow councils to decide on their own governance arrangements, including a return to the committee system where demanded.

Signposts for reform

This is no mere tealeaf-reading exercise. As the Widdicombe report argued, British local government has no independent right to exist, not least because of the sovereignty of Parliament and the unwritten constitution. While this maxim continues to hold sway, it is doubtful that any government would seek to sweep aside centuries of traditions of local representation. However, local government's power continues to decline as more complex forms of governance give oversight to local public services, with the scrutiny role being pushed as a new duty in lieu of the oversight once enjoyed. Even on the basis of the dividing lines of the duopoly Labour and Conservative parties at Westminster, it is doubtful that the 'localism' they profess will ever see a return to fully fledged local self-government, never mind the seemingly almost (by British standards) utopian concept of 'general competence'. Local government itself finally appreciates this and has mounted a last defence against encroaching centralism in the form of seeking to better the reputation of local councils, realising that their unpopularity in some quarters hinders its defence as a political institution. The under-performance and perceived irrelevance of local government will continue to be held up as a justification for any reform or enactment by the centre perceived to be an erosion of local democracy. For all the reforms imposed on local government by the centre – from executive arrangements and scrutiny to Best Value and CPA – expecting enthusiasm for culture shift and increased performance could be said to be akin to expecting a patient to perform a surgical procedure on themselves. Problems within the machinery of government at the centre do not help matters much either. Only since 2002 has local government had its own department in Whitehall, languishing prior to this in a single division of several ever-changing super-ministries. As such, the considerable sway of the Treasury over both policy debate and spending has demonstrated itself over local government more than most other public services.

Since 1997, New Labour have been largely successful in securing the constitutional change promised by their election manifestos, from devolution to Scotland and Wales and removing the hereditary peers from the Lords, through to the Human Rights and Freedom of Information Acts (though not a referendum on electoral reform for the Commons). Their failure to deliver elected regional assemblies in England outside London was not for want of trying, eventually. However, the party's appetite for constitutional reform has diminished since entering government for the third time in 2005, as evidenced by the limited number of proposals in the manifesto that year. Minor reforms are tabled for Scotland and Wales in the light of the experience of devolution and this section will consider the unfinished business for sub-national government in England. This agenda may also pick up again once the Blair era comes to its natural end; after all, even the Conservatives are considering their own reform package not entirely aimed at unpicking New Labour's achievements in this area, having accepted devolution. The government has stated that it has no plans to attempt to reintroduce elected regional assemblies, though it has not proposed the dismantling of the regional structures introduced in anticipation of them. Instead, the agenda has moved on to city regions, spurred on by the distinct lack of competitiveness between English cities and their European counterparts and the appreciation of their role as economic drivers of regional economies, which even the OECD has acknowledged. Indeed, the dividing line between Blairites and Brownites appears to be the willingness to devolve powers to new city regions rather than just relying on the almost traditional regional development agencies to deliver on this. At one point, the emerging thinking from the Brown camp appeared to suggest favouring retaining the current myriad of local councils and grafting boards on top of these to administer funding streams, i.e. rebranded centralism. No doubt this would prove popular with most local councillors but reform appears to be very much back on the agenda. Some members of the Brown camp apparently hold out hope for the resumption of moves towards elected regional assemblies, with the attendant reorganisation of two-tier shire England this would entail. It is highly probable that a future Conservative government would dismantle the existing regional structures outside London, though what state local government will be by that point is a different matter. While the Conservatives have come around to the city regional agenda themselves to some extent, the onus here is on voluntary co-operation between existing bodies rather than top-down new structures, not sharing the prescriptive approach argued for by the likes of the Centre for Cities.

Leaving aside the already discussed city regional agenda, the generational opportunity to settle the question of what size and shape local government in England should resemble constantly rears itself. Even in Scotland and Wales, where unitary local government is barely a decade old, mergers are being discussed in the name of efficiency, in spite of the large size of some local councils already. The recent reforms in Northern Ireland, where the number of councils and councillors have been reduced to make way for streamlined governance and a more professionalised representative, may point the way for the rest of the UK. Similarly, in London with its thirty-two unitary boroughs (the oldest councils in Britain, technically) and the mostly co-operative arrangements between them and the GLA, reform is sometimes raised. The 2006 revisions to the London Plan by the mayor saw the boroughs grouped together in five sub-regions, leading some to comment that the mayor's agenda for five super-boroughs (each the size of Birmingham) is back for debate. Even the City of London Corporation, historically the most adept local authority at avoiding reform, has re-emerged as a candidate for reform once more, with the possibility of a commuter vote as the final undeniable answer to its conundrum of how to introduce democracy to a council which serves hardly any residents. Labour continues to show no interest in voting reform for local government (compared to the historic advocacy by the Liberal Democrats) and the Conservatives remain implacably opposed to the mere suggestion, despite their continuing lack of representation in northern cities such as Manchester and Newcastle under first past the post.

The past three decades have seen constant managerial reform and the divisions between the parties on this reduced to almost microscopic size, especially since many of the issues the Tories have objected to (CPA, for instance) will be largely irrelevant by the time of the next election, while structural reform may already be in train and unstoppable by that point also. For the time being at least, the sun appears to have set on the ambition of some ministers to introduce single-service elected bodies, which manifested itself in 2003 with the consideration by the Home Office of elected police authorities but was ultimately rejected by Labour, though it could return again under the Conservatives. It is not only the Home Office but also local public services who must demonstrate how they are 'fit for purpose'. Similarly, the question of how to finance local government, the last ideological divide here, may be settled by this point, with the Lyons Review having reported on not only this but also the size and shape of local government and its new role as a 'place shaper'. In a decade's time, local government may have been shorn of its existing role in education and social services, leaving councils as local 'liveability' agencies to look after the street scene and fight anti-social behaviour on the ground. Local government reform in Scotland through electoral reform was instigated only at the behest of the Liberal Democrats as a pre-condition of going into co-operation with Labour; any demands to enact their radical agenda for local government as part of a deal at Westminster in the event of a hung Parliament would be diluted substantially in comparison, though this represents the only possible deviation from this script. It simply remains to ask: where is there left to go now for local government? Positively no stone has been left unturned.

Appendix I

Useful contacts

Local Government Association and others

Local Government Association (www.lga.gov.uk)
The LGA, formed on 1 April 1997, promotes the interests of English and Welsh local authorities – a total of just under 500 authorities.

Confederation of Scottish Local Authorities (www.cosla.gov.uk)
The representative voice of Scottish local government, also acting as the employers' association on behalf of all thirty-two Scottish unitary councils.

Northern Ireland Local Government Association (www.nilga.org)
NILGA was established in October 2001, replacing the Association of Local Authorities for Northern Ireland, and represents the province's twenty-six district councils.

Welsh Local Government Association (www.wlga.gov.uk)
The WLGA represents the interests of local government and promotes local democracy in Wales. It represents the twenty-two local authorities in Wales, and the four police authorities, three fire and rescue authorities and three national park authorities are associate members.

Centre for Public Scrutiny (www.cfps.org.uk)
The CfPS provides best practice and guidance to local authorities in relation to their scrutiny role.

Improvement and Development Agency (www.idea-knowledge.gov.uk)
The IDeA was created in 1999 (alongside the Employers' Organisation) from the former Local Government Management Board as a clearing house for best practice in relation to both local authority services and elected members.

Local Authorities Coordinators of Regulatory Services (www.lacors.gov.uk)
Set up in 1978 to co-ordinate the enforcement activities of trading standards, LACORS provides advice and guidance to help support local authority regulatory and related services. Since 1991, it has also worked on food safety and is currently responsible for a range of other regulatory and related services.

Local Authorities Research & Intelligence Association (www.laria.gov.uk)
LARIA was established in 1974 to promote the role and practice of research within the field of local government and provide a supportive network for those conducting or commissioning research.

National Association of Local Councils (www.nalc.gov.uk)
Established in 1947, NALC represents some 10,000 parish and town councils in England and community councils in Wales at the non-principal tier.

Central government

Department for Communities and Local Government
(www.communities.gov.uk)
The DCLG was created in May 2006 with a powerful remit to promote community cohesion and equality, as well as responsibility for housing, urban regeneration, planning and local government.

Audit Commission (www.audit-commission.gov.uk)
With commissioners appointed by the DCLG, the Audit Commission is an independent public body responsible for ensuring that public money is spent economically, efficiently and effectively, in the areas of local government, housing, health, criminal justice and fire and rescue services.

Boundary Committee for England (www.lgce.gov.uk)
Established on 1 April 2002, the Boundary Committee is a statutory committee of the Electoral Commission and has assumed the functions of the Local Government Commission for England. It is responsible for recommendations for changes to local authority electoral arrangements and their implementation.

Commission for Social Care Inspection (www.csci.gov.uk)
Launched in April 2004, the CSCI is the single independent inspectorate for all social care services in England.

Leadership Centre for Local Government (www.lg-leadership.gov.uk)
The Leadership Centre works with local authorities in England to develop the quality of leadership among their political leaders and officers.

Local Government Ombudsmen (www.lgo.org.uk)
The Local Government Ombudsmen investigate complaints of injustice arising from maladministration by local authorities and certain other bodies. There are three Local Government Ombudsmen in England and they each deal with complaints from different parts of the country.

Office for Standards in Education (www.ofsted.gov.uk)
The inspectorate for children and learners in England, Ofsted was created in 1993 as the reconstituted Office of HM Chief Inspector of Schools.

Standards Board for England (www.standardsboard.co.uk)
The Standards Board for England helps build confidence in local democracy. It does so by promoting the ethical behaviour of members and co-opted members who serve on a range of authorities through receiving and investigating allegations that members may have breached the code of conduct.

Chartered institutes and institutes

Chartered Institute of Environmental Health (www.cieh.org)
Founded in 1883 as the Association of Public Sanitary Inspectors, the institute regulates the profession as well as contributing to the development of policy around public health and safety.

Chartered Institute of Housing (www.cih.org)
Formed as the Institute of Housing Managers from a merger of the Society of Housing Managers and the Institute of Housing in 1965, what became the Institute of Housing in 1974 received its Royal Charter in 1984 and changed its name to the Chartered Institute of Housing in

1994. It is the professional body for those working in public and social housing.

Chartered Institute of Library and Information Professionals
(www.cilip.org.uk)
The institute was formed in 2002 from the merger of the Library Association and the Institute of Information Scientists. It regards itself as the leading professional body for librarians, information specialists and knowledge managers working across the public sector.

Chartered Institute of Public Finance and Accountancy
(www.cipfa.org.uk)
CIPFA works across the public sector to govern the public accountancy profession and contribute to the development of policy, working with the government on a range of financial issues.

Chartered Institution of Wastes Management (www.iwm.co.uk)
The CIWM is the professional body for waste and resource management.

Institute of Leisure and Amenity Management (www.ilam.co.uk)
ILAM is the professional body for the leisure industry and represents the interests of leisure managers across all sectors and specialisms of leisure.

Institute of Public Rights of Way Management (www.iprow.co.uk)
Established in 1986, IPROW is the professional body that represents individuals who are involved in the management of public rights of way in England, Wales, Scotland and Northern Ireland.

Institute of Revenues Rating and Valuation (www.irrv.org.uk)
The IRRV exists to support the professional and personal development

and the sharing of best practice of those working in its three fields.

Institute of Sport and Recreation Management (www.isrm.co.uk)
Formed as the Association of Bath Superintendents in 1921 and subsequently the Institute of Baths and Recreation Management, the ISRM supervises the professional conduct and development of those working in sports and leisure on behalf of local authorities.

Institution of Civil Engineers (www.ice.org.uk)
The Institution of Civil Engineers was founded in 1828 and represents the interests of professionals working in the built environment.

Royal Town Planning Institute (www.rtpi.org.uk)
The RTPI exists to advance the science and art of town planning for the benefit of the public.

Trading Standards Institute (www.tsi.org.uk)
The TSI (formerly the Institute of Trading Standards Administration) is a professional association formed in 1881. It represents trading standards professionals in the UK and overseas, in local authorities, in the business and consumer sectors and in central government.

Associations and societies

Association of Council Secretaries and Solicitors (www.acses.org.uk)
ACSeS is the professional body representing those chief officers and their deputies (in principal local authorities in England and Wales) who are responsible for the management of legal and administrative functions. It came into being in 1996 with the merging of the Association of District Secretaries and the Society of Council Secretaries.

Association of Directors of Social Services (www.adss.org.uk)
The ADSS represents all the directors of adults' social services and directors of children's services in England, Wales and Northern Ireland.

Association of Electoral Administrators (www.aea-elections.co.uk)
Founded in 1987, the association was set up as the professional body to represent the interests of electoral administrators in the United Kingdom.

Association of Town Centre Management (www.atcm.org)
The ATCM is the leading organisation in Europe concerned with managing and improving town and city centres.

Bar Association of Local Government and the Public Service (www.balgps.org.uk)
The BALGPS is a direct successor of the Society of Local Government Barristers, which had been in existence since about 1945, and of the Bar Association for Local Government, which had been formed in 1977.

British Association of Social Workers (www.basw.org.uk)
The BASW is the largest association representing social work and social workers in the UK.

Chief Culture and Leisure Officers Association (www.cloa.org.uk)
The professional body for directors and senior managers of local authority leisure and cultural services.

County Surveyors' Society (www.cssnet.org.uk)
Established in 1885, the CSS is the national body for those engaged in surveying, transportation studies, traffic management and road safety.

LG Communications (www.lgcomms.org.uk)
LG Communications (formerly the Society of County and Unitary Public Relations Officers) represents local authority public relations and communications teams across the United Kingdom.

National Governors' Association (www.nasg.org.uk)
Formed in 2006 from the merger of the National Governors' Council and the National Association of School Governors, the NGA is an organisation for school governors run by school governors.

Planning Officers Society (www.planningofficers.org.uk)
The POS was formed in April 1997 by the amalgamation of the former County Planning Officers Society, the District Planning Officers Society and the Metropolitan Planning Officers Society.

Public Sector People Managers' Association (www.ppma.org.uk)
Formerly the Society of Personnel Officers, the PPMA is the organisation which represents and serves the professional interests of its public sector people management members, providing them with continuing professional development, knowledge and information, a network/forum - and advice for raising professional standards in people management.

Society of Chief Librarians (www.goscl.com)
The SCL is a professional association made up of the chief librarians of each library authority in England, Wales and Northern Ireland.

Society of County Treasurers (www.sctnet.org.uk)
The SCT comprises of all county council chief financial officers.

Society of Information Technology Management
(www.socitm.gov.uk)

SocITM was founded in 1986 as the professional association for ICT managers working in and for the public sector.

Society of Local Authority Chief Executives and Senior Managers (www.solace.org.uk)
SOLACE is the representative body for senior strategic managers working in local government. It promotes effective local government and provides professional development for its members.

Solicitors in Local Government (www.slgov.org.uk)
SLG is a professional association which represents the 4,000 local government solicitors and trainees in England and Wales.

Regional government and city regions

Core Cities (www.corecities.com)
Comprising Birmingham, Bristol, Leeds, Liverpool, Manchester, Newcastle, Nottingham and Sheffield, the Core Cities group represents England's eight provincial capitals in discussions with government and policy makers.

England's Regional Development Agencies
(www.englandsrdas.com)
The national secretariat of England's regional development agencies.

English Regions Network (ern.smartregion.org.uk)
The ERN is the umbrella organisation for England's eight regional assemblies.

Northern Way (www.thenorthernway.co.uk)
Led by three regional development agencies, the Northern Way aims to

connect the north's eight city regions to bring about economic prosperity for their people.

Passenger Transport Executive Group (www.pteg.net)
PTEG represents the six passenger transport executives of Greater Manchester, Merseyside, South Yorkshire, Tyne & Wear, West Midlands and West Yorkshire. Strathclyde Partnership for Transport and Transport for London are associate members.

Think tanks

Centre for Cities (www.ippr.org.uk/centreforcities)
The Institute for Public Policy Research's Centre for Cities is an independent urban policy research unit which looks at how UK cities function.

Centre for Local Economic Strategies (www.cles.org.uk)
CLES is an independent organisation involved in regeneration, local economic development and local governance. It brings together a network of organisations, including regeneration partnerships, local authorities, regional bodies, community groups and voluntary organisations.

GreenSpace (www.green-space.org.uk)
GreenSpace is a registered charity set up to help those committed to the planning, design, management and use of public parks and open spaces.

Living Streets (www.livingstreets.org.uk)
Living Streets are champions of streets and public spaces for people on foot, working on practical projects to create safe, vibrant and healthy streets for all.

Local Government Information Unit (www.lgiu.gov.uk)
The LGIU is an independent policy and research think tank. It provides information, advice, training and lobbying, representing the interests of local authorities and supporting them in delivering excellent results for their communities.

New Local Government Network (www.nlgn.org.uk)
The NLGN was founded in 1996 by a small group of senior local government figures whose stated aim was to make local government more relevant and credible to local people. A non-profit-making, independent think tank, the NLGN seeks to transform public services, revitalise local political leadership and empower local communities.

Office for Public Management (www.opm.co.uk)
The OPM is an independent, not-for-profit, public interest company, working with people to develop high quality management, professional practice and public engagement in organisations that aim to improve social results.

Public Management and Policy Association (www.pmpa.co.uk)
The PMPA has been successfully helping managers, policy makers and academics keep in touch with and understand the wider cross-cutting developments in public policy making that affect the governance, general and financial management of public services since June 1998.

Town and Country Planning Association (www.tcpa.org.uk)
The TCPA is an independent campaigning charity calling for more integrated planning based on the principles of accessibility, sustainability, diversity, and community cohesion. It puts social justice and the environment at the heart of the debate about planning policy, housing and energy supply.

International

Cities Alliance (www.citiesalliance.org)
Cities Alliance is a global coalition of cities and their development partners committed to scaling up successful approaches to poverty reduction.

Commonwealth Local Government Forum (www.clgf.org.uk)
The CLGF was founded in 1995 as a focus for action on local democracy in the Commonwealth and was endorsed by Commonwealth heads of government at their meeting in New Zealand that year.

Conference of Atlantic Arc Cities (www.arcat.org)
Representatives of cities from Europe's Atlantic coast wishing to develop an area of solidarity and projects.

Council of European Municipalities and Regions (www.ccre.org)
The Council of European Municipalities was founded in Geneva in 1951 by a group of European mayors; later, it opened its ranks to the regions and became the CEMR.

Eurocities (www.eurocities.org)
Founded in 1996, Eurocities is a network of more than 120 large cities in more than thirty European countries.

United Cities and Local Governments (www.cities-localgovernments.org)
UCLG aims to be the united voice and world advocate of democratic local self-government, promoting its values, objectives and interests, through co-operation between local governments, and within the wider international community.

Academic

Cardiff School of City and Regional Planning (www.cardiff.ac.uk/cplan)

Centre for Local and Regional Government Research, Cardiff University (www.clrgr.cf.ac.uk)

Centre for Suburban Studies, Kingston University (fass.kingston.ac.uk/research/centres/suburban_studies/index.shtml)

Centre for Urban and Community Research, Goldsmiths, University of London (www.goldsmiths.ac.uk/cucr)

Centre for Urban and Regional Development Studies, University of Newcastle upon Tyne (www.ncl.ac.uk/curds)

Centre for Urban and Regional Governance, University of Westminster (www.wmin.ac.uk/sshl/page-950)

Centre for Urban Policy Studies, University of Manchester (www.sed.manchester.ac.uk/geography/research/cups)

Centre for Urban Research, London School of Economics (www.lse.ac.uk/collections/urbanresearch)

European Services Strategy Unit (www.european-services-strategy.org.uk)

Institute of Local Government Studies, University of Birmingham (www.inlogov.bham.ac.uk)

Institute for Political and Economic Governance, University of Manchester (www.ipeg.org.uk)

Regional Studies Association (www.regional-studies-assoc.ac.uk)

Sustainable Cities Research Institute (www.sustainable-cities.org.uk)

Media

First (www.lga.gov.uk/first)

Local Government Chronicle (www.lgcnet.com)

MJ (www.municipalyearbook.co.uk)

New Start (www.newstartmag.co.uk)

Planning and *Regeneration & Renewal* (www.regenerationmagazine.com)

Appendix II

Key legislation

1979–83: Conservatives' first term

1980 Education Act
Allowed for parent school governors and parental choice of schools

1980 Local Government Planning and Land Act
Introduced the right to buy for council housing, competitive tendering, urban development corporations and block grants

1982 Local Government Finance Act
Established the Audit Commission and abolished supplementary rates

1983–7: Conservatives' second term

1984 Rates Act
Introduced rate capping

1985 Housing Act
Extended the right-to-buy scheme and set habitation standards

1985 Local Government Act
Abolished the Greater London Council and the six metropolitan county councils

1985 Local Government (Access to Information) Act
Allowed public access to council committee meetings and papers

1986 Housing and Planning Act
Further extended the right-to-buy scheme and allowed transfer of housing stock to a social landlord

1987–92: Conservatives' third term

1988 Education Reform Act
Introduced local financial management in schools and the right of schools to opt out of local authority control; removed polytechnics from LEA control

1988 Housing Act
Created Housing Action Trust areas to renovate local authority housing stock

1988 Local Government Act
Made competitive tendering compulsory

1988 Local Government Finance Act
Introduced the community charge (or poll tax) to England and Wales and centralised business rates collection

1989 Children Act
Reformed local authority children's services

1989 Local Government and Housing Act
Introduced political restriction for senior local government officers and the requirement to allocate council committee places on an electorally proportionate basis; banned council rent subsidies

1990 Environmental Protection Act
Empowered local authorities to regulate the local environment

1990 National Health Service and Community Care Act
Removed local authority representation on local health authorities

1990 Town and Country Planning Act
Empowered local authorities to require developers to provide local facilities when granting planning permission, among other reformed powers

1992–7: Conservatives' fourth term

1992 Food Act
Empowered local authorities to inspect premises used to prepare and sell food

1992 Further and Higher Education Act
Removed local further education and sixth form colleges from LEA control

1992 Local Government Act
Created the Local Government Commission to review structures in order to move towards a unitary pattern of local government

1993 Leasehold Reform, Housing and Urban Development Act
Extended the right-to-buy scheme and gave the right to repairs for council tenants

1993 Trade Union Reform and Employment Rights Act
Allowed for the privatisation of local careers' services

1994 Local Government (Scotland) Act
Reformed Scottish local government into thirty-two unitary authorities

1994 Local Government (Wales) Act
Reformed Welsh local government into twenty-two unitary authorities

1994 Police and Magistrates' Courts Act
Reduced local authority representation on police authorities by half

1996 Housing Act
Reformed the social rented sector, including registration of social landlords

1997–2001: Labour's first term

1997 Local Government (Contracts) Act
Confirmed the power of councils to arrange for the private provision of services and to enter into contracts

1997 Local Government Finance (Supplementary Credit Approvals) Act
Enabled local authorities to release capital receipts

1997 Local Government and Rating Act
Increased the powers of parish councils and removed business rates exemption from Crown property

1998 Crime and Disorder Act
Established a statutory role for local authorities in community safety

1998 Government of Scotland Act
Created a devolved Scottish Parliament, including overall responsibility for local government

1998 Government of Wales Act
Created a devolved Welsh Assembly, including the powers of the Secretary of State for Wales over local government

1998 Human Rights Act
Ratified the European Convention on Human Rights into UK law, affecting all public bodies

1998 Public Interest Disclosure Act
Protected whistleblowers against loss of employment from reporting corruption

1998 Regional Development Agencies Act
Established eight regional bodies for strategic and economic planning in England

1998 School Standards and Framework Act
Established education action zones; reformed opt-out schools; allowed local ballots on the future of local selective schools; allowed ministers to take over failing LEAs and individual schools

1999 Greater London Authority Act
Established the Greater London Authority, defining the powers of the office of mayor of London and a 25-member London Assembly elected under proportional representation

1999 Local Government Act
Abolished general capping and introduced the Best Value regime

2000 Freedom of Information Act
Provided a statutory right of access to information and a duty for local authorities to publish information

2000 Learning and Skills Act
Established local learning and skills councils with local authority representation; abolished local training and enterprise councils; extended OFSTED inspection to further education and sixth form colleges

2000 Local Government Act
Required local authorities to promote the economic, social and environmental wellbeing of their areas; introduced the duty to publish community strategies; introduced new standards arrangements; abolished the surcharge; introduced new executive management arrangements, including the option of having a directly elected mayor if approved by a local referendum

2001–5: Labour's second term

2001 Health and Social Care Act
Required local authorities to consider the activities of local health service provision in their overview and scrutiny function

2002 National Health Service Reform and Health Care Professions Act
Abolished community health councils

2003 Local Government Act
Allowed prudential borrowing by local authorities; created business improvement districts; repealed the Section 28 ban on educating on homosexuality issues in schools

2003 Regional Assemblies (Preparations) Act
Empowered the Secretary of State to order referendums in each region on the question of whether or not to have an elected regional assembly for that region; allowed the Boundary Committee for England to enact reviews of local councils in order to recommend unitary patterns for any region assenting to an assembly

2004 Children Act
Integrated children's services within local authorities and established children's trusts

2004 Housing Act
Reformed the powers of local housing authorities, particularly with regard to private rented accommodation and housing standards, including long-term empty properties

2004 Planning and Compulsory Purchase Act
Simplified the planning system; increased community involvement; sped up inquiries into major developments; removed Crown immunity from the planning process; regionalised spatial planning

2005 Clean Neighbourhoods and Environment Act
Enabled local authorities to improve the quality of the local environment by providing new powers for them to deal with a range of anti-social behavioural issues such as fly-tipping, graffiti and litter

2005 Education Act
Reformed school funding arrangements by allowing for three-year budgets and guaranteed levels of funding from central government to schools

(Note: Parliamentary sessions may not correspond with election dates and are given as a general chronological guide)

Appendix III

2005 general election manifestos

Conservative

Best Value and inspection: abolish Best Value and CPA.

Council Tax: retain council tax, abolish capping and introduce pensioner discount.

Regional governance: scrap entirely outside London and pass functions to county councils, allow London Assembly more powers to hold London mayor to account and scrap proportional representation for its elections.

Other: scrap the Office of the Deputy Prime Minister, introduce elected sheriffs.

Labour

Best Value and inspection: continue Best Value regime and reform CPA while streamlining the number of inspectorates.

Council tax: retain council tax until Lyons inquiry reports on reform options, retain capping and introduce three-yearly funding for local authorities to ensure stable finances.

Regional governance: retain existing regional assemblies and development agencies (but no plans to reintroduce elected regional assemblies), review powers of London mayor.

Other: new powers for neighbourhoods over regeneration and anti-social behaviour and four-yearly local elections.

Liberal Democrats

Best Value and inspection: abolish inefficient inspection regimes and make Audit Commission stronger and more independent by merging all inspectorates.

Council tax: scrap the council tax and replace with a system of local income tax while allowing councils more freedom over spending.

Regional governance: replace regional quangos with democratic oversight by local councils in each region.

Other: electoral reform for local councils, allow councils to decide their own governance arrangements and introduce the power of general competence for all local authorities.

Appendix IV

Key dates

April 1974

Local government reorganisation outside London: new structure introduced of 6 metropolitan counties and 39 shire counties, divided into 36 metropolitan and 296 non-metropolitan districts.

Responsibility for water and sewerage transferred to water authorities.

Ambulance and some health services transferred to health authorities.

March 1981

Merseyside Development Corporation established.

July 1981

London Docklands Development Corporation (LDDC) established.

April 1985

London Regional Transport transferred from the local authority sector.

April 1986

Abolition of Greater London Council and metropolitan county councils. In London, functions transferred to City of London, London boroughs, the Inner London Education Authority (ILEA), the London Fire and Civil Defence Authority (LFCDA), the London Waste Regulation Authority (LWRA), waste disposal authorities and other bodies such as the London Planning Advisory Committee. In metropolitan areas, functions passed to metropolitan districts, waste disposal authorities (in Merseyside and Greater Manchester) and joint authorities for police, fire and civil defence, and transport. Residuary bodies were set up to wind up the affairs of the abolished councils.

October 1986

Responsibility for municipal bus services transferred to public transport companies.

April 1987

Responsibility for municipal airports (except Manchester) transferred to public airport companies.

May 1987

Black Country, Teesside, Trafford Park and Tyne and Wear Development Corporations established.

April 1989

Funding of polytechnics and higher education colleges transferred to the Polytechnics and Colleges Funding Council.

City technology colleges and one City College for the Technology of Arts established in fifteen local education authorities (until 1993) as independent specialist schools.

Sept 1989

The first grant-maintained schools come into existence following the 1988 Education Reform Act. These schools are independent of local authority control. They are funded by central government through the Funding Agency for Schools. Part of local authority expenditure on education consists of payments back to the government for the funding of these schools.

April 1990

ILEA abolished. Responsibility for education in inner London transferred to the twelve inner London boroughs.

March 1992

Birmingham Heartlands Development Corporation established.

July 1992

Local Government Commission set up to review the structure of local government in England.

April 1993

Local authorities become responsible for implementing new legislation on community care.

Funding of colleges of further education and sixth form colleges transferred from local authorities to the Further Education Funding Council.

May 1993

Plymouth Development Corporation established.

July 1993

Careers service functions transferred from local authorities to local partnerships approved by the Secretary of State.

April 1995

Isle of Wight unitary authority replaces the county council and two district councils. New police authorities set up in the shire areas, taking all policing responsibilities away from county councils.

April 1996

Unitary authorities created in Avon, Cleveland, Humberside and North Yorkshire, replacing both shire districts and Avon, Cleveland and Humberside county councils. New combined fire authorities created in each of these four authorities. Waste regulation becomes the responsibility of the Environment Agency, resulting in the abolition of the LWRA.

April 1997

Unitary authorities created in Bedfordshire, Buckinghamshire, Derbyshire, Dorset, Durham, East Sussex, Hampshire, Leicestershire, Staffordshire and Wiltshire, replacing some of the shire districts in these areas. New combined fire authorities also created in these areas.

April 1998

Unitary authorities created in Berkshire, Cambridgeshire, Cheshire, Devon, Essex, Hereford and Worcester, Kent, Lancashire, Nottinghamshire and Shropshire, replacing some shire districts and Berkshire County Council. New combined fire authorities were also created in each of these areas.

Urban development corporations outside London abolished and

assets transferred to the Commission for the New Towns (later English Partnerships).

June 1998
LDDC abolished.

April 1999
Funding of grant-maintained schools transferred to local authorities; city technology colleges permitted to remain independent if choosing to do so.

July 2000
Greater London Authority created, consisting of a directly elected mayor and a separately elected assembly, and four functional bodies. The four functional bodies are:

   i. The Metropolitan Police Authority, overseeing policing in London (excluding the City). An entirely new local authority, the Receiver for the Metropolitan Police having been abolished.
  ii. The London Fire and Emergency Planning Authority, essentially a reconstitution of the old LFCDA.
 iii. Transport for London (TfL), which has strategic responsibility for transport in London; TfL also has responsibility for London buses and is the highway and traffic authority for certain major roads in the capital.
  iv. The London Development Agency, promoting economic development and regeneration in London.

April 2002
Funding of sixth form education transferred from local authorities to the Learning and Skills Council.

July 2003
Control of London Underground transferred from the Department for Transport to TfL.

October 2003
Thurrock Urban Development Corporation established.

April 2004
Combined fire authorities in shire areas become major precepting authorities, having previously been financed by payments from the county or unitary councils in their area.

May 2004
London Thames Gateway Development Corporation established.

July 2004
Strategic planning transferred from county councils to regional planning bodies/regional assemblies under regional spatial strategy reforms.

December 2004
West Northamptonshire Urban Development Corporation established.

March 2005
New Forest National Park comes into existence.

April 2005
Responsibility for magistrates' courts transferred from local authorities to Her Majesty's Courts Service.

Bibliography

A. Alexander, *The Politics of Local Government in the United Kingdom* (London: Longman, 1982)

H. Atkinson and S. Wilks-Heeg, *Local Government from Thatcher to Blair* (Cambridge: Polity Press, 2000)

S. Bailey, *Local Government Economics* (Basingstoke: Macmillan, 1999)

R. Berg and N. Rao (eds), *Transforming Local Political Leadership* (Basingstoke: Palgrave Macmillan, 2005)

T. Byrne, *Local Government in Britain: Everyone's Guide to How It All Works*, 7th ed. (London: Penguin, 2000)

J. Chandler, *Local Government Today*, 3rd ed. (Manchester: Manchester University Press, 2001)

M. Chisholm, *Structural Reform of British Local Government: Rhetoric and Reality* (Manchester: Manchester University Press, 2000)

A. Cochrane, *Whatever Happened to Local Government?* (Buckingham: Open University Press, 1993)

C. Copus, *Party Politics and Local Government* (Manchester: Manchester University Press, 2004)

B. Denters and L. Rose (eds), *Comparing Local Governance: Trends and Developments* (Basingstoke: Palgrave Macmillan, 2005)

S. Duncan and M. Goodwin, *The Local State and Uneven Development: Behind the Local Government Crisis* (Cambridge: Polity Press, 1988)

P. Dunleavy, *Urban Political Analysis: The Politics of Collective Consumption* (London: Macmillan, 1980)

H. Elcock, *Local Government: Policy and Management in Local Authorities*, 3rd ed. (London: Routledge, 1994)

D. Farnham and S. Horton (eds), *Managing the New Public Services*, 2nd ed. (Basingstoke: Macmillan, 1996)

R. Fenney, *Essential Local Government 2002* (London: LGC Information, 2002)

S. Goss, *Making Local Governance Work: Networks, Relationships and the Management of Change* (Basingstoke: Palgrave, 2001)

J. Gyford, S. Leach and C. Game, *The Changing Politics of Local Government* (London: Unwin Hyman, 1989)

R. Hale and Anna Capaldi (eds), *Councillors' Guide to Local Government Finance* (London: CIPFA, 2005)

W. Hampton, *Local Government and Urban Politics*, 2nd ed. (London: Longman, 1991)

D. Hill, *Democratic Theory and Local Government* (London: Allen and Unwin, 1974)

D. Hill, *Urban Policy and Politics in Britain* (Basingstoke: Macmillan, 2000)

P. Houlihan, *The Politics of Local Government: Central–Local Relations* (Harlow: Longman, 1986)

G. Jones (ed.), *The New Local Government Agenda* (Hemel Hempstead: ICSA, 1997)

G. Jones and J. Stewart, *The Case for Local Government*, 2nd ed. (London: Unwin Hyman, 1985)

D. Judge, G. Stoker and H. Wolman (eds), *Theories of Urban Politics* (London: Sage, 1995)

D. King and G. Stoker (eds), *Rethinking Local Democracy* (Basingstoke: Macmillan, 1996)

J. Kingdom, *Local Government and Politics in Britain* (Hemel

Hempstead: Philip Allan, 1991)

R. Leach and J. Percy-Smith, *Local Governance in Britain* (Basingstoke: Palgrave, 2001)

S. Leach, H. Davis *et al.*, *Enabling or Disabling Local Government: Choices for the Future* (Buckingham: Open University Press, 1996)

S. Leach, J. Stewart and K. Walsh, *The Changing Organisation and Management of Local Government* (Basingstoke: Macmillan, 1994)

S. Leach and D. Wilson, *Local Political Leadership* (Bristol: Policy, 2000)

M. Loughlin, M. Gelfand and K. Young (eds), *Half a Century of Municipal Decline 1935–1985* (London: Allen and Unwin, 1985)

B. Lucas and P. Richards, *A History of Local Government in the Twentieth Century* (London: Allen and Unwin, 1978)

A. McConnell, *Scottish Local Government* (Edinburgh: Edinburgh University Press, 2004)

J. Newman, *Modernising Governance: New Labour, Policy and Society* (London: Sage, 2001)

C. Pearce, *The Machinery of Change in Local Government 1888–1974: A Study of Central Involvement* (London: Allen and Unwin, 1980)

B. Pimlott and N. Rao, *Governing London* (Oxford: Oxford University Press, 2002)

N. Rao, *The Making and Unmaking of Local Self-Government* (Aldershot: Dartmouth, 1994)

N. Rao, *Reviving Local Democracy: New Labour, New Politics?* (Bristol: Polity, 2000)

P. Richards, *The Local Government System* (London: Allen and Unwin, 1983)

S. Snape and P. Taylor (eds), *Partnerships between Health and Local*

Government (London: Frank Cass, 2004)

J. Stewart, *The New Management of Local Government* (London: Allen and Unwin, 1986)

J. Stewart, *The Nature of British Local Government* (Basingstoke: Macmillan, 2000)

J. Stewart, *Modernising British Local Government* (Basingstoke: Palgrave Macmillan, 2003)

J. Stewart and G. Stoker (eds), *The Future of Local Government* (Basingstoke: Macmillan, 1989)

J. Stewart and G. Stoker (eds), *Local Government in the 1990s* (Basingstoke; Macmillan, 1995)

G. Stoker, *The Politics of Local Government*, 2nd ed. (London: Macmillan, 1991)

G. Stoker (ed.), *The New Politics of British Local Governance* (Basingstoke: Macmillan, 2000)

G. Stoker, *Transforming Local Governance* (Basingstoke: Palgrave Macmillan, 2004)

G. Stoker and D. Wilson (eds), *British Local Government into the 21st Century* (Basingstoke: Palgrave Macmillan, 2004)

M. Taylor, *Public Policy in the Community* (Basingstoke: Palgrave Macmillan, 2003)

T. Travers, *The Politics of Local Government Finance* (London: Allen and Unwin, 1986)

T. Travers, *The Politics of London: Governing an Ungovernable City* (Basingstoke: Palgrave Macmillan, 2003)

T. Travers and G. Jones, *The New Government of London* (York: Joseph Rowntree Foundation, 1997)

D. Wilson and C. Game, *Local Government in the United Kingdom*, 3rd ed. (Basingstoke: Palgrave, 2002)

K. Young and N. Rao, *Local Government since 1945* (Oxford: Blackwell, 1997)

Index